BALANCING THE BASICS

A HANDBOOK FOR TEACHERS OF READING (K-8)

Trevor Cairney

Ashton Scholastic

Sydney • Auckland • New York • Toronto • London

Other Books by Trevor Cairney
Write-on Books (with R. Ingle)

National Library of Australia
Cataloguing-in-Publication data

Cairney, Trevor.
  Balancing the basics.

  Bibliography.
  Includes index.
  ISBN 0 86896 238 4.

  1. Reading (Elementary). I. Title.

372.4'14

First published in 1983 by Ashton Scholastic Pty Limited (Inc. in NSW), PO Box 579, Gosford 2250. Also in Brisbane, Melbourne, Adelaide, Perth and Auckland, NZ.

Illustrated by John Deacon.

Typeset by InterType Pty Ltd, Surry Hills, NSW.

Printed by Bridge Printery Pty Ltd, Rosebery, NSW.

6 5 4 3 2

CONTENTS

PREFACE

This book, as the title suggests, is basically an ideas book for teachers interested in fostering the reading skills of their pupils. However, unlike most teachers reference books, which examine skill development, this book attempts to show that these skills can be developed without reducing reading purely to a series of isolated activities.

The general approach suggested reflects a philosophy stressing that the teaching of reading should primarily proceed *from whole to part* and should always have, as its ultimate aim, *a search for meaning*. This viewpoint has been arrived at both by working with children and by studying the complex nature of the reading process.

Reading obviously requires the reader to use many linguistic, perceptual and cognitive processes. Many children master these processes simply through experience of language and reading. However, all children need some help to develop and use these processes at various stages in their development, and a small proportion of children (who experience reading difficulties) require a great deal of assistance. To provide this assistance, teachers need to be aware of both the specific processes and the various subskills that are a part of them. This knowledge provides a focus for instruction and allows teachers to introduce children to specific subskills within the context of 'real' reading.

This book therefore aims to sensitise teachers to the many subskills and processes that are important in reading. It is hoped that these ideas will make it easier to respond quickly to the needs of each child, and to implement effective teaching programs.

Acknowledgement

I wish to thank my friend and colleague Robert Ingle for his interest in this manuscript and for the constructive criticism he has offered.

CHAPTER ONE
Introduction

Probably no aspect of reading instruction has created more controversy than skill development. Can reading be broken up into separate subskills? Can hierarchies of subskills be outlined? Can reading subskills be taught? Indeed, should reading subskills be taught? These are some of the questions that have been asked.

There is no simple answer to any one of these questions, and research evidence has hardly been conclusive. Unfortunately, the evidence has led very much to a polarisation of views, with ranks being drawn and forces marshalled on two opposing fronts: one camp supporting the teaching of reading by the systematic treatment of identified subskills; and the other suggesting an holistic approach, which views subskills as something that can be learnt only incidentally as the child is given the opportunity to read regularly.

It is probably worth noting that often the most extreme viewpoints have been held by people who have very rarely had to tackle the problem classroom teachers face every day: that of developing the reading ability of a large class of children.

Classroom teachers have often been the losers in the continued philosophical debate between the 'skillers and drillers' and the supporters of holistic approaches. Many teachers have found it difficult to know just what to do. Many have felt the need for skill development and believed that they have an important part to play in this process, but the form that this role should take in the process of skill development has often been unclear to them.

Holistic supporters see the teacher's role as that of an adviser giving help when the need appears, as part of normal everyday reading—but this is a role that many teachers find unworkable. Little wonder, then, that many of them have been unsure of what they should do.

The stance taken in this book is that, while reading should be learnt predominantly *from whole to part*, there is a limited place for skill development, which proceeds from part to whole. For example, in my work with beginning readers it has often been patently obvious that some children make more rapid initial progress if introduced to a number of words in isolation before commencing the reading of sentences. While I have introduced many young children to reading using a language experience approach, it seems clear that this does not work for *every* child. The children who did make rapid progress were usually children who already possessed sound concepts of what letters, sounds and words were. The children who failed to learn using a language experience approach were usually the children who did not possess these concepts and who did not easily grasp them when confronted with whole sentences. It appears that these children needed first to be able to see the parts before they could deal with the whole.

My experience has led me to believe that a more realistic view of skill development is that, while many skills will be acquired simply by providing children with frequent opportunities to experience **real reading** (i.e. reading for meaning), there are times when the teacher needs to adopt positive strategies that will aid this development. However, it must be stressed that this skill development should occur within the context of real reading, not as a series of isolated exercises. Reading subskills should never become the focus for all instruction.

The reading process

Increasing awareness of the complexity of the reading process has helped to create even further debate concerning the place of skills within the reading program.

Interest in the reading process has grown rapidly in the past fifteen years. One of the greatest stimuli for this interest has been the increasing participation of psychology and linguistics in reading research, and the knowledge gained from the merging of these two disciplines.

Several models have been proposed, each of which seems to have added something to our growing knowledge of the reading process. However, the viewpoints expressed have often differed markedly.

The models developed have tended to form a continuum, ranging from those with a heavy code emphasis to those with a heavy meaning emphasis. At the code emphasis end of the continuum, researchers (e.g. La Berge and Samuels, 1974; Gough, 1976) have conceptualised reading as a process involving letter-by-letter and word-by-word processing. These models assume that the reader derives meaning from a text by first decoding the print, then processing this input in a linear way through various knowledge levels. These models have been called **bottom-up models**. Generally, supporters of code emphasis models have tended to follow a structured skills-in-isolation approach to reading instruction, while those supporting meaning emphasis models have usually adopted an holistic approach to skill development.

At the meaning emphasis end of the continuum, researchers (e.g. Goodman, 1973; Smith, 1973; Kolers, 1972; Neville and Pugh, 1977; and Levin and Kaplan, 1970) have suggested that high-level cognitive processes interact with and direct the flow of information through the lower level processes (e.g. decoding skills such as letter recognition). Furthermore, they have assumed that efficient readers are actively engaged in hypothesis testing as they proceed through a text, sampling print to test their initial hypotheses. These models have been called **top-down models**.

The Goodman model

The most widely accepted model of the reading process in the last decade has been that outlined by Kenneth Goodman. Goodman (1976) argues that the prime purpose of reading is to reconstruct meaning: 'without meaning it simply is not reading'. He views reading as a communication process between writer and reader that is similar in many ways to the communication between speaker and listener.

In fact, while accepting that there are obvious differences between oral and written language (e.g. oral language is used in context, whereas for written language the writer must create context), Goodman suggests that written language is a parallel form of oral language.

Furthermore, Goodman stresses that language is learnt in the context of experience, and that readers re-create meaning by associating experiences (and the concepts formed as a result of these) with language.

Thus, Goodman suggests that, in effect, reading is a 'psycholinguistic guessing game', in which the reader uses three major sources of information:

Grapho-phonic information　This includes:
* graphic information (e.g. letters, spelling, patterns, spacing);
* phonological information (i.e. sounds and sound patterns created through intonation); and
* phonic information (i.e. sound–symbol relationships).

Syntactic information　This includes:
* sentence patterns (i.e. grammatical sequences);
* pattern markers (i.e. function words, e.g. *in*, *the*; inflections that convey grammatical information, e.g. *ing*; and punctuation); and
* transformational rules, which are supplied by the reader in response to the perceived surface structure, and help him/her to reach the deep structure meaning.

Semantic information　This includes the reader's:
* experience;
* concepts (existing concepts help to shape meaning); and
* vocabulary, which helps him/her to draw upon experiences and concepts in response to specific words.

In the Goodman model, it is suggested that all these sources of information are used simultaneously and interdependently. The reader uses just enough graphic information, in combination with semantic and syntactic information, to extract meaning from print. At times an initial letter may be all that is necessary to identify a word in order to complete a sequence or confirm a prediction. The following example illustrates how this process occurs:

> Jason was a member of the winning cricket team. Throughout the competition he had been one of the best players. As a bowler he had managed to take thirty-five wickets. He bowled 150 overs, including thirty-four maidens.

When reading this short paragraph, a reader with a sound knowledge of cricket has a clear advantage. His personal experience and knowledge of cricket concepts and vocabulary (e.g. overs, wickets, maidens, bowled) – semantic information – provide a great source of information, which makes it easier for him to extract meaning from the print.

A non-cricketer reading the final sentence may stumble over the word *maiden*. He may attempt to predict the word, using his knowledge of sentence patterns – syntactic information – but without sufficient semantic knowledge he will struggle. He will probably expect a noun, but which one? Clearly, he needs to use far more graphic information than the cricketing reader.

Even after looking carefully at the word and realising that it is *maiden*, the non-cricketer will probably still be confused. He may know about maidens, but he can be forgiven for wondering how they fit into this strange sport. The cricketing reader, on the other hand, probably requires far less graphic information, perhaps only sampling the initial letter.

Goodman thus sees reading as an active process in which the reader uses many different cues to help to construct the meaning being communicated by the author. The efficient reader (like the efficient listener) engages in a language process involving sampling, predicting, testing and confirming, thus relying on strategies that yield the most reliable prediction with the minimum use of information available (Goodman, 1973, p. 23).

Recent developments in reading research

In recent years, much research has been conducted to test whether top-down models validly represent the reading process, and also to explore further the many ideas raised by researchers like Goodman.

Probably, the most dramatic growth has occurred in our understanding of the knowledge sources that Goodman has broadly labelled 'semantic' cues. While Goodman stresses the importance of semantic information in the reading process, he does not elaborate the specific nature of this information. Recent research has shown more precisely the great variety of semantic knowledge available to the reader. This research has shed new light upon the nature of the reading process, by clearly outlining the specific nature of the strategies and knowledge sources that Goodman claims are operative.

The knowledge sources identified can almost be outlined in an hierarchical fashion, ranging from high level processes operating at contextual level (e.g. schemata) to lower level processes operating at word level (e.g. semantic components of words).

Schemata   Rumelhart (1980), for example, has attempted to apply the concept of schemata (plural of schema) to the field of reading. A **schema** is a concept used to describe how knowledge is represented. It is a structure for representing concepts stored in memory. Rumelhart suggests that we possess schemata that make it easier to store and retrieve knowledge relating to objects, situations, events, actions and sequences of actions.

However, it should not be assumed that schemata are simply stored data structures. As Iran-Nejad (1980) has stressed, they are really constantly changing, coherent masses of ideas and concepts aroused by some interest or purpose.

A central function of schemata appears to be to aid comprehension. It seems that, when the reader is confronted with a text and attempts to construct meaning, his/her interpretation is shaped by relevant schemata. Even before commencing to read a text, he/she begins to draw upon relevant schemata.

For example, confronted with a story title like 'Daryl Scores Again', the reader may immediately start drawing upon relevant schemata concerning games (e.g. soccer, football) and how they are played. When considered with *again*, these may also make him/her think of the glory and adulation of being a sports star and all that this entails. Of course, depending upon individual experience, a completely different set of schemata may be activated.

Once the reader starts reading, his/her initial hypotheses are either confirmed or rejected, and additional schemata are retrieved to aid processing. In effect, one schema can activate further schemata, some of which may be embedded within the original schema. The reader will then comprehend the text to the extent that he/she is able to retrieve schemata that help to construct a coherent representation of the author's message.

Scripts   A number of other researchers have attempted to shed further light on the comprehension process, with the concept of scripts. A **script** is a detailed list of events (in sequence) that characterise a specific situation. It includes a list of roles for characters within a specific situation.

It has been claimed that scripts, like story grammars (see below), exist as intuitive knowledge, enabling the reader to understand specific parts of a text by relating them to a situational stereotype.

Schank (1975) has demonstrated the function of scripts with the following simple example:

Feeling hungry, John went into a restaurant. The waiter brought him the menu.

Schank points out that, for the reader to integrate these two sentences, additional knowledge must be used, and that scripts are one such source of semantic knowledge. Schank suggests that these sentences will activate a restaurant script, which will expand the rather limited domain of reference supplied by the text. The reader will be able to use his/her knowledge of expected roles, props and actions in a restaurant to fill out the text. For example, a lot must occur between the time John enters the restaurant and the moment the waiter hands him the menu. The concept of scripts helps us to understand how the reader is able to infer this unwritten information.

Story grammars   It has also been suggested that readers use internalised story structures or plans to aid comprehension (Rumelhart, 1980; Mandler and

Johnson, 1977; Stein and Glenn, 1977; Thorndyke, 1977). These schematic representations of stories have been labelled **story grammars**.

It appears from the research done, that previous experience of reading and hearing stories helps the reader to develop an intuitive awareness of the structure of stories. This knowledge in turn helps to increase the predictability of reading material, thus increasing his/her comprehension of it.

Anaphora   A closer examination of elements at both the word and sentence level has also provided interesting insights into the type of semantic information used while reading. For example, a great deal of new knowledge has been obtained concerning the elements and devices in a story that help to give it a sense of cohesiveness. One such device is anaphora.

Anaphora is a concept used to describe elements in a story that make the reader refer back to something read before. One single word in a story can evoke in the reader's mind a complex chain of events making him/her refer back to previous events or ideas in the text. For example:

> Frederick was an excellent fisherman. He never seemed to stray far from the water. However, while he was good at *it*, he didn't enjoy it.

In this short piece of text, the word *it* evokes in the reader's mind the concept 'fishing'. A mature reader is able to infer quite easily that what Frederick does not like is fishing, even though fishing is not mentioned anywhere in the text. Thus, this simple anaphora acts to bind the various elements of the text together, which in turn aids comprehension.

Semantic components of words   Even at the level of individual words, new insights have been gained concerning the semantic information that readers use.

Vocabulary knowledge has always been accepted as an important factor to consider when discussing reading. Measures of vocabulary have consistently been shown to have a close relationship to reading comprehension. The reasons for this close relationship have caused great conjecture.

However, while debate has continued over these wider issues, researchers have become increasingly more interested in studying the 'depth' of understanding that can be associated with vocabulary knowledge.

It is now widely accepted that a word can be represented as a bundle of semantic components (Bierwisch, 1970). For example, the stimulus of a single word like *gramophone* leads the reader to think of the semantic components: record player, machine, manually powered, old, etc.

As might be expected, it has been found that children seem to have more global meanings for words than adult readers, and more limited knowledge of the semantic components of words. It seems that there is a growing differentiation of word meanings with age and experience (Anderson and Freebody, 1979).

It appears that the infinite number of semantic components indicated by specific words in context also influence the meaning obtained from a story.

An updated view of the reading process

All of the above research has further confirmed the fact that reading is indeed a complex process requiring the co-ordination and use of many different information sources. It seems that reading is a multilevel interactive process that requires the reader to analyse texts at various levels (ranging from a single letter to the whole text). As well as processing the explicit features of the text, the reader must also bring a great deal of pre-existing knowledge to the reading process. The interaction of knowledge-based and text-based processes is essential to reading comprehension. Thus, reading is an inferential constructive process, characterised by the formation and testing of hypotheses concerning the reader's perceptions of the author's intended message.

It seems that, for skilled readers, both top-down processing and bottom-up processing are occurring at all levels of analysis simultaneously while he/she reads. It seems logical that, while adults may use both processes concurrently with few problems, young readers or children experiencing reading problems may not do this. It may well be that beginning readers will fail to apply either of these strategies efficiently. On the other hand, they may rely too heavily on one at the expense of the other.

There is obvious danger in relying too heavily on bottom-up processing, as the young reader does if subjected to an unchanging diet of poorly constructed and heavily controlled texts, or if he/she experiences a purely phonic approach to reading. In cases like these, the search for meaning is lost as the child struggles to cope with every detail of the print.

However, it is just as serious for the reader to rely too heavily on top-down processing. In this case, the child is guessing wildly, with little understanding of the author's intended message.

Obviously, there must be a proper balance between the information the reader brings to the text and the information the text provides for the reader.

Clearly, reading depends on many linguistic, perceptual and cognitive processes. From the moment the reader makes the decision to read, a large number of these processes come into play. This may best be illustrated with a simple example:

A proficient reader who is also a football fanatic picks up the Monday morning newspaper and turns to the sports page. How may the reading process unfold?

While turning to the back page, the reader immediately starts to retrieve relevant schemata (i.e. those relevant for football) and to make predictions (i.e. formulate hypotheses for testing) (e.g. Will the Arrows beat the Hawks? Will the Bombers lose their third consecutive game?). To make these predictions, he must draw on relevant background knowledge (e.g. the Bombers beat the Hawks in the first round; the Bombers were playing the competition leaders).

As the reader's eyes hit the page, the headline *Bombers Crash Again* is immediately noticed. He derives almost instant meaning from these words with limited sampling of print. Perhaps he scans only the first syllable of *Bombers*, maybe none of *again*. He already knows that the Bombers were beaten in both their previous games, so obviously they have been beaten *again*. The word *again* is redundant in view of his existing knowledge.

The reader's eyes may then move quickly to the game score at the end of the article, which immediately tells him whether it was an easy victory or a close game. In turn, each of these possible outcomes would stimulate the retrieval of different schemata and scripts leading to further hypotheses (e.g. Dazzler Dan played another good game for the Arrows; Coach Cratty again failed to motivate the Bombers).

The reader then moves back to the beginning of the article, to commence searching for print that will help to confirm or reject these hypotheses.

As the reader proceeds to sample print, he progressively creates meaning. This is done by using a combination of grapho-phonic information (i.e. he samples print at word level, e.g. an initial letter or a single morpheme), syntactic information and semantic information. This then activates further knowledge sources (e.g. semantic components stimulated by a single word; a script to help make sense of a sequence of events, such as a script concerning the scoring of a try in rugby; or a pronoun that, with the aid of inference, suggests a referent in a previous paragraph). These higher-level knowledge sources help him to create new hypotheses, which in turn are tested by sampling further print.

In this way the reader progressively reconstructs the meaning the newspaper reporter has attempted to communicate.

While this example involves the reading of a newspaper, it appears that similar strategies are used in most reading situations. Certainly, the interactive manner in which the various strategies are used will be similar for most reading.

An acceptance of the above viewpoint concerning the nature of the reading process justifies the approach suggested at the beginning of this chapter concerning the development of reading skills.

Developing reading skills

If we accept that the reading process is an active thinking process involving the interaction of text-based processes, there are a number of clear implications for the development of reading skills:

• It should be remembered that the term 'reading skill' should not be restricted simply to decoding skills. Many different strategies and knowledge sources are used by the readers.

• Many reading skills are possessed intuitively by readers and develop naturally through their experience of language and reading.

• Readers need to be able to use both bottom-up and top-down processes when reading. Problems arise when children either lack specific skills or are unable to co-ordinate the many skills and knowledge sources necessary to derive meaning from print. Your role is to intervene when this occurs, to help overcome the child's problems.

• Reading skills are never applied in isolation; rather, they are used in an interactive way as the reader searches for meaning. Therefore, children should be given the opportunity to develop skills in the context in which they will ultimately be used. This does not deny that some children may require a different approach; however, reading skills should generally be taught in the context of 'real' reading.

Such an approach to skill development is a demanding one and requires you to respond quickly to the perceived needs of children. It also rests heavily on the assumptions that:

• you have the time to identify individual needs; and
• you have the knowledge and experience to diagnose accurately the child's weaknesses or readiness for a higher order skill.

While there *are* teachers who have an intuitive awareness of exactly what each child needs, and of where he/she has to go, for many, this is 'easier said than done', given the constraints and pressures evident in every classroom.

How this book can help

The outline of reading skills and activities in this book is included to heighten your awareness of the need to help each child to develop reading skills. It is offered as an aid to help you to identify in children a focus for instruction, so that you can plan and implement programs that develop and extend every child in your care.

I feel that such a list is useful, and perhaps essential for many teachers, to enable you:

• to identify what children already know;
• to decide what you can and *should* teach;
• to decide when it is appropriate to introduce a specific skill;
• to decide how you can develop this skill, in the context of 'real' reading;
• to teach skills to individuals and groups of children who have similar needs.

Dangers   Despite these good intentions, there are many dangers involved in the publication of such a list. The main ones to beware of are:

• Do not succumb to the impression that each skill in a skills list has a separate identity, because in reality all skills are highly interrelated. For example, while understanding various concepts of print (i.e. what is a word, letter, sound) is listed as separate skills, do not assume that these skills are learnt separately. Clearly, they are acquired concurrently as the child is involved in the sharing of books.

• Do not attempt to teach these skills by providing children with isolated activities.

• Do not interpret any sequence included as an indication that all children should learn these skills in precisely this order. The absurdity of this assumption can be seen by observing the phonic knowledge rapidly acquired by beginning readers as they commence reading. No two children learn exactly the same units in exactly the same order.

• Do not overlook the fact that most skills can be treated at a number of different levels. To use the term 'mastery' is a little dangerous, because it is virtually impossible at times to say with any certainty that a child has mastered a specific skill. Perhaps he/she has mastered it at 'that level' in relation to 'that specific activity', but it is difficult to assume more.

Take, for example, the single comprehension skill of finding the main idea. At a simple level, it can be performed by a five-year-old asked to supply a title for a picture; at a more difficult level, a ten-year-old may struggle when asked to find the topic sentence in a specific paragraph.

The skills   In spite of all these problems and dangers, an attempt is made in the following chapters to outline specific skills in a loosely arranged sequence. Many will criticise this attempt and ask for the research evidence that has led to such a sequence. Obviously, no such research evidence is available, nor perhaps ever will be available. This is because the order in which skills are acquired is variable, and because, as already mentioned, they can be 'mastered' at many different levels. There is little need for researchers to continue searching for the elusive optimum sequence, because it simply does not exist.

The sequence here is included only because to list skills randomly would be to deny that some skills are more difficult than others, and that some are prerequisites for more difficult skills that follow.

The skills and activities specified are based on my experience with many children of all ages, the limited research information that is available, and the observations of the many outstanding teachers with whom I have worked. They are included only as a guide. *No list of skills can do more.*

The activities   The inclusion of specific activities is, I feel, essential; it is an attempt to provide even further guidance. Many published skills lists are useless because they provide little indication of what the skills mean in terms of child performance. An outline is given of activities that are appropriate to teach each skill. All these activities are designed to be used in the context of real reading. In this sense the stance taken in this book is an holistic one, although clearly it includes a slightly different view of your role in the development of reading skills.

Obviously, there are two ingredients in the secret of success with such an approach:
• Know your children.
• Be aware of some of the many skills that are important for reading.

The skills and activities that follow are outlined in the hope that they will help you to identify individual needs clearly and to implement appropriate strategies to satisfy them.

For simplicity, these skills and the appropriate activities are grouped into four main categories:
• reading readiness (Chapter 2);
• word identification (Chapter 3);
• comprehension (Chapter 4); and
• reading for a variety of purposes (Chapter 5).

CHAPTER TWO
Reading readiness

The very mention of the word 'readiness' often causes debate between reading educators and teachers. The concept itself is probably best described as a developmental stage children (supposedly) reach, which is characterised by the mastery of a number of specific skills seen as necessary prerequisites for reading.

Traditionally, it has been assumed that children reach this stage somewhere between the ages of five and six years (Gates, 1937). The first year of schooling has often been viewed as a period important for the development of reading readiness.

However, in recent years reading research (Durkin, 1972) has shown that the practice of delaying children's introduction to reading has been based upon a number of misconceptions:

• It is possible to assess readiness using a checklist of basic skills. In reality, many of the skills identified have little direct relationship to reading (e.g. an absence of hunger, good balance, willingness to share, ability to tie shoelaces, emotional security).

• It is possible to recognise objectively a point at which children are ready to read. (This is difficult to pinpoint accurately.)

• Reading is mainly a visual process.

• Visual and auditory perception can best be developed by providing sequences of carefully graded discrimination exercises.

• The perception of likenesses and differences between objects, pictures and patterns is directly related to the ability to discriminate between letters and words.

Obviously, there are a number of visual and auditory skills that children do require to read successfully. However, it appears that the best way to develop these skills is by actually beginning reading. In most cases the development of reading readiness, and beginning reading, should be the same thing.

Many teachers delay the commencement of reading because they feel that, if a child lacks the necessary visual and auditory skills, failure will result, which in turn may have a disastrous effect upon the child's confidence.

This is quite a sensible argument, and in part I agree with it. However, in many cases failure need not result. Furthermore, if failure does result, it is often caused not by a lack of readiness, but by an incorrect approach to early reading.

A procedure I have found successful for both beginning reading and developing reading readiness is as follows:

Step 1   From the very first day, turn every lesson into a language lesson. Constantly talk to children, and encourage them to talk to you (and each other).

Step 2   Read good literature to them several times a day. Let them see you turning pages, pointing to words and discussing pictures. There is no need to structure lessons; just read.

Step 3   Commence a daily writing program from the very first week. At first, many will draw; some will scribble; others will make rhythmic patterns; some will write their names; a few will write words. Even just scribbling in their blank books will help children to develop important concepts (e.g. a book has a front and a back; pages should be used in a specific sequence). The work of Clay (1975) and Graves (1981), as well as the observations of many teachers, has shown (not surprisingly) that children learn a great deal about reading by composing their own written messages.

Step 4   Within the first few weeks of school, begin to surround them with print. Remember, they have been living in a world full of print for five years. Attach meaningful labels to things of interest around the room. Take a few minutes to read these each day — together at first, but later let individuals read them.

Step 5   Provide first-hand experiences for children, and record these experiences so that you can read about them later. Take a few minutes several times a day to read something you have written. Send some of this reading material home.

Step 6   While carrying out steps 1–5, begin to provide special skills lessons designed to ensure that children can discriminate between different letters and words. Seize upon their discoveries about print to reinforce their knowledge of the relationship between letters and sounds.

You should find that many children will not need these lessons; but if they do, do not be afraid to provide them.

Step 7   Teach a few sight words. You may disagree with this strategy, but it is often necessary, in order to make children more aware that sentences are, in fact, composed of separate words. This concept is obviously essential for reading. Start with a few nouns; next introduce some structural words (e.g. *this, and*); then introduce a couple of common verbs. Further details concerning these procedures are provided in Chapter 3.

If some children have problems at this stage, give them more of steps 1–6.

Step 8   Create stories for them, using words you know that they can read. Try to make the stories as meaningful as you can. This step will often be needed for only a few weeks. It will boost confidence and reinforce necessary skills (e.g. understanding what a word is, and the idea of left-to-right sequence).

Step 9   Provide caption books for children to read — their first 'real' books.

This is not the only possible approach, but it is one that has worked for me.

The most important point to remember is that all children are at different stages of development when they arrive at school. Unfortunately, it is not always realistic to assume that every child can be allowed to find his/her own starting point. However, it *is* realistic to group children broadly within the classroom, so that they can be extended fully.

Steps 1–5 are relevant for all children. However, whether all children will need step 6 (most will), or whether some can jump straight to steps 7, 8 and 9 is a decision you will need to make, based on your knowledge of individual children.

The following readiness skills are included purely as a guide. Their inclusion is designed to make you more aware of the skills that are relevant to beginning reading. Many of these skills will develop quite naturally as children are surrounded by print; others will, at times, require a little reinforcement.

Never assume that children cannot commence reading until they have mastered these skills. Providing children with the opportunity to experience reading is the best way to develop 'readiness' skills. If this is done in an informal way, and draws heavily upon children's language and experience, you should experience few problems.

For convenience, these skills are broken into a number of categories, but do not assume that they should be developed in isolation. In fact, the only way effectively to develop these skills is by adopting an integrated approach.

Language skills

While it cannot be said that the following abilities are prerequisite skills for reading, it is quite clear that they are important skills for reading. Children enter school possessing most of these abilities to some extent. They are included here to heighten your awareness of the need to continue their development as an integral part of the beginning-reading program.

SKILLS

- Recalling the meaning and function of words that will eventually be seen in print
- Understanding a variety of common sentence patterns
- Determining the meaning of a word within an orally presented sentence, by using context clues
- Understanding that words have different meanings when used in a variety of contexts

ACTIVITIES

⭐ **Language experience activities** The easiest and most effective way to develop all these abilities is by providing first-hand experiences as a starting point for integrated language activities. Often, experiences arise spontaneously and can act as a springboard for language. However, at other times *provide* experiences for children. These may be:
  * growing vegetables;
  * cooking;
  * having a dress-up day;
  * experimenting with shadows;
  * holding a treasure hunt;
  * providing taste experiences; and
  * planning major excursions.

• Relating personal experience to messages presented orally (e.g. understanding the word *punt*, because of having travelled across a river on one)

• Understanding the relationship between speaking, listening, reading and writing

• Understanding that print conveys meaning

• Understanding that stories have form and structure beyond sentence level (i.e. that a story is made up of a series of sequenced events)

These experiences will provide opportunities for children to:
* talk;
* compose stories (which you scribe for them);
* publish these stories in class books; and
* share the stories with other children.

✪ **Read constantly to children** It has consistently been observed that children who live in a home rich in literature seem to commence reading earlier and make more rapid progress. The discussion concerning the reading process in Chapter 1 provides additional support for the importance of literature. It seems that reading aloud to children is important for several reasons:

* It helps to increase their knowledge of language patterns.
* It leads to a growth in their vocabulary.
* It is the easiest way to convince them that books can be a source of enjoyment.
* It can help to broaden the knowledge of children who may have had limited experiences, because it enables them to step outside their own culture and to experience things through the eyes of others.
* It helps you to get closer to them (which is perhaps one of the key characteristics of a successful teacher).
* It helps to develop important listening skills and the ability to concentrate for an extended period of time.
* It broadens their knowledge of the structure of language and stories.

There are only a few rules to remember:
* Read often (five-year-olds should have several short sessions each day).
* Select a wide variety of material (including poetry and plays).
* Let children watch you reading when possible (with large print books, run your finger under the words for all to see as you read).

✪ **Writing** Provide children with an opportunity to experience writing as soon as they enter school (as discussed earlier). By writing about their own experiences (using invented spelling at first), children can learn a great deal about the link between written and spoken language. One of the most rewarding features of early writing programs is that children show great willingness to talk about their writing to everyone. In this sense, writing is also a tremendous stimulus for language.

✪ **Special language activities**   The following ideas also have proved useful for me with young children:

Group story telling   This is an exciting activity. Begin by making up a start to a story (e.g. 'One cold and foggy morning, while walking to school, I stumbled across ...'), then allow children to continue. Each child quickly adds a piece to the story as you move around the group.

Feelie bags   Place an object in a bag, then ask individual children to feel the object through the bag and describe its shape, size, texture, etc. Other children try to guess what it is.

Wordless picture books   This is very similar to the above activity, but it is a little easier, because children slowly build up a story based on the pictures provided.

Describing things   Ask children to describe art, games, craft objects, etc.

Sequencing picture cards   (and composing a simple story to go with them) A good extension to this activity is to allow children to create the last picture in the sequence.

Picture talks   These can be limiting, but with an exciting picture and sensible teacher questioning they can still be useful.

Puppetry   This is always an outstanding activity; it often allows children to use language more freely.

Riddles, poems and songs   Sharing these helps both memory and language development.

Role playing   This may follow a moral dilemma story or may arise quite spontaneously.

Retelling stories   After telling a story, ask children to retell it. Perhaps allow them to do it in groups, with each member taking responsibility for one part.

Special topics   The use of special topics can also be quite useful (e.g. 'The strangest pet', leading from a discussion of children's own pets).

Concepts of print

While separate print concepts are identified below, do not assume that these should be taught separately. All these skills will develop naturally if children are provided with a rich experience of print and books. The approaches outlined are considered to be the most appropriate.

SKILLS	ACTIVITIES
• Holding a book the right way up • Identifying the cover of a book • Understanding the difference between print and pictures • Understanding that print can be matched to spoken language • Understanding the concepts of **word**, **letter** and **sound**	✪ Read to children daily. Children of five–six years of age should probably be read to several times a day. Before reading, clearly indicate the cover (perhaps discuss the pictures and read the title), then proceed to read each page, pointing to each as you read. Perhaps also point to the print as you read, smoothly running a finger beneath the words. Children may hold the book and turn the pages for you. ✪ Provide shared book experiences. This involves applying many of the above points to large versions of a book. Many of these books are now available commercially, although some

• Processing print from left to right (which involves understanding page sequence, word sequence and letter sequence)
• Processing a page of print from top to bottom

teachers prefer to produce their own books that are copies of favourite picture books.
✪ Produce language experience books, which are then shared with children.
✪ Provide integrated reading–language activities. Many activities can readily be planned to translate the language of children into print:
    * Surround children with labels and captions using meaningful phrases (e.g. *Enter at your own risk*; *Finger-eating fish*). Further ideas for labelling and captioning are provided in Chapter 3.
    * Read nursery rhymes (or television jingles).
    * Dramatise words and phrases.
    * Make a class message board and leave a message each day (e.g. *Darren gets the lunches today*). Read each message with children.
    * Help children to prepare class books on special topics (e.g. 'Tastes I like', 'Soft things', 'Green things', 'I can …').

Auditory skills

In many books, auditory skills sections are divided into **gross discrimination** and **fine discrimination**. Gross discrimination often includes skills such as discriminating between environmental sounds, percussion instruments, artificial sounds, voices, and sounds that vary in pitch, volume and tempo. While these skills may be prerequisites for fine discrimination, I have usually found that most children arrive at school having mastered them. There seems little point in including them here. However, there are a number of discriminatory skills that some five-year-olds do require help with from time to time, and these are given in the outline that follows.

Also given are a number of memory skills that seem to be of some importance for reading.

SKILLS

Auditory discrimination
• Discriminating fine differences in sound between rhyming words

ACTIVITIES

✪ Reading and reciting poetry are an ideal way to develop this ability. Reading many children's books with predictable rhyme (e.g. Dr Seuss books) is also very useful.
✪ Perhaps try a cooperative cloze exercise with poems. Read the material, but leave specific words out; children suggest possible alternatives. Well-known nursery rhymes are a fun

• Identifying words that are the same or words that are different

• Identifying words with specific initial, final and medial sounds

Auditory memory

• Recalling and reproducing verbal directions

• Recalling and reproducing simple rhymes, jingles and songs
• Recalling and reproducing language units of increasing length and complexity

• Recalling and reproducing sequences of events from a story

way to start (e.g. *Tinkle, tinkle broken jar* ...).

✪ Read lists of four to six words with only one word different. Ask children to indicate which word was different (e.g. bun, bun, run, bun).

✪ Present pairs of words, and ask children to indicate whether they are the same or different.

✪ Ask children to listen while you read and to identify words with specific sounds (e.g. 'Put your hand up every time you hear a word starting with *t* [sound]').

✪ For fun, read lists of words, and ask children to pick the word that has a different initial, final or medial sound.

✪ Give children a series of verbal instructions, and see whether they can follow them (e.g. 'Bring me the big green book from the second shelf').

✪ Nursery rhymes, television jingles, songs, number rhymes and riddles are all useful to help develop auditory memory.

✪ **Shopping game** Let children pretend that they are compiling a shopping list, to which each child in turn adds an item. Each child must remember all previous items and add another. Continue until someone forgets an item.

✪ **Echo game** Divide children into two groups, one standing on each side of the room. In unison, one side calls out sentences that the other side has to repeat (more softly, like an echo).

✪ **Story repetition** Following a story, ask children to remember and repeat special phrases (e.g. 'Run, run as fast as you can, you can't catch me I'm the Gingerbread Man. I got away from a little old woman and ...').

✪ After reading a story, ask children to draw a sequence of pictures in answer to specific questions (e.g. 'Of what did the first little pig build his house?', 'Of what did the second little pig ...?', 'What was the first animal to chase the Gingerbread Man?', 'What was the second ...?'). The pictures should illustrate the general story line.

• Recalling and reproducing messages	✹ Ask children to take a message to another room.
	✹ Pass a message around the classroom.

Visual skills

Reading readiness programs and checklists also often include visual skills that are of little use in any reading program. Many of these skills (e.g. perceiving likenesses and differences between objects, pictures, shapes, designs and sequences of shapes) have very little to do with the ability to identify words or larger language units. Research has shown that there is very little relationship between these discriminatory skills and being able to read. In any case, from my experience it seems that very few children enter school unable to find the rabbit with the missing ear or the dog with three legs. However, the discriminatory skills given in the outline that follows do appear to have some relationship to the ability to read (although some even question this assumption).

Further, some include recalling and/or reproducing details from pictures, objects, position of objects, sequences of pictures and visual images as necessary memory skills. While these skills are obviously useful, they are not included in the outline, because I feel that many children need very little work in these skills and that, once again, the relationship between these skills and reading is tenuous.

SKILLS	ACTIVITIES
Visual discrimination	
• Perceiving a word as a complete unit (form perception)	✹ Many advocate using jigsaws and picture and pattern completion as valuable prerequisite activities for the perception of words. While these appear to be worthwhile activities, the relationship between the skills involved and the perception of words is tenuous. Activities that appear to have a more direct relationship are:
	* Ask children to point to the separate words in a shared book experience.
	* Ask children to find words in a grid of letters.
	* Ask children to complete words (e.g. *d-g, litt-e*).
• Perceiving likenesses and differences between words in terms of form, direction and internal differences	✹ Ask children to circle the word that is different in a group of words (e.g. *dog, dig, dog, dog*).
	✹ Ask children to circle the incorrect form of a word (e.g. *girl, girl, gril, girl*).
	✹ Ask children to match pairs of words (or phrases) that are the same (flashcards are useful).

• Copying letters and words

✪ Play Snap or Fish, using word or phrase cards.

✪ Once again, many teachers advocate the copying of patterns, shapes and designs prior to the use of words. This seems quite unnecessary. In most cases, words are no more difficult to copy than patterns. It is more useful to ask children to copy:

  * single letters or sequences of letters; and
  * words, using plastic letters, plasticine, pencil and paper, chalk, etc.

• Perceiving a specific letter or word in a variety of forms and contexts

✪ Ask children quickly to scan a page (or sentence) to find a specific word.

✪ Ask children to find and circle specific words in a grid of letters.

✪ Show children a set of words written in a variety of print types, with variations also in colour and size. Ask them to circle a specific word whenever it is written. Environmental words are excellent for this purpose.

Visual memory

• Recalling and/or producing letters and words

✪ Show children a sequence of letters, remove it, then ask them to reproduce the sequence, using plastic letters or pencil and paper.

✪ Show a sequence of words (flashcards or written on the board), remove one card, then ask children to indicate which word was removed.

✪ **Concentration game** This game (played with flashcards) is simple and a lot of fun. Select ten to twenty pairs of cards (two for each word). Lay cards face down in a grid pattern. Allow children to turn cards over one at a time. If a child can recall where another word the same is located, he/she keeps the pair. The game continues until all words are gone. It can be played with two to six children.

CHAPTER THREE
Word identification

This area of reading has been surrounded by much confusion in recent years. Psycholinguistic research has rightly shown that there is a lot more to reading than decoding and recognising individual words. Clearly, the most frequently used strategy of proficient readers is **contextual analysis**. This refers to the use of semantic and syntactic information to predict exactly what a word is. It is more a thinking process than a set of discrete skills to be learnt.

However, contextual analysis is rarely used alone. Typically, it is used in association with other word identification skills, namely:
- word recognition skills;
- phonic analysis; and
- structural analysis.

Each of these skills has an important part to play. The relative importance of each of them varies depending upon the type of material to be read, as well as the child's stage of reading development. Beginning readers, for example, appear to require the use of more visual information than proficient readers. While some reading educators deny this and claim that the strategies the beginning reader uses are exactly the same as those used by adults, it appears from my teaching experience that, irrespective of the approach used to introduce children to reading, they tend to require additional visual information, at least in the initial stages.

This is hardly surprising. We would logically expect adults, after years of reading experience, to be able to recognise instantly far more words than the beginning reader, and their understanding of the inconsistencies and consistencies of sound–symbol relationships to be extensive. We would also expect proficient readers to be able to sample print more efficiently than beginning readers and thus to require less use of strategies such as word recognition, phonic analysis and structural analysis.

While it is probably true that the best way for children to learn how to sample print efficiently is by experiencing real reading, it also appears that, at times, beginning readers need to focus their attention on the intricacies of print.

Beginning readers need initially to be shown that sentences are composed of separate word units, which, when recognised instantly, make reading easier. They also need to be shown that single letters or groups of letters can provide quick cues for identifying words in context.

However, you should not initially teach children to read by systematically introducing them to individual sounds and words in isolation. You should immediately give them the opportunity to see that the main function of reading is to obtain meaning. The use of word identification skills, other than contextual analysis, should be encouraged within the context of complete texts.

Remember that, in relation to reading, the meaning contained within a whole sentence or passage is not simply the sum of its parts.

Word recognition

A distinction should be made between **word recognition** and **reading vocabulary**. Word recognition refers to the ability to recognise a word instantly, whereas reading vocabulary refers to the reader's knowledge of the meanings of words. Word recognition work is concerned with the core of common words that frequently occur in our written language. These are usually referred to as **sight words**.

Remember that, just because a word is recognised, it does not follow that the child necessarily understands the meaning of the word. For this reason, reading educators have sometimes criticised reliance upon word recognition skills. It has been argued that, since reading involves a search for meaning, there is little point in relying too heavily upon word recognition skills. Furthermore, it has been argued that there is little point in teaching children to recognise words in isolation, because, in reality, the meaning of words varies greatly in context.

However, to reject word recognition skills would be to deny that some visual information is important for reading. Quite clearly, the ability to identify whole words instantly is a valuable strategy in attempting to obtain meaning from print.

Proficient readers can recognise tens of thousands of words instantly; this *in part* enables them to use fewer visual cues when reading. Beginning readers obviously have far more limited word-recognition skills. While, quite rightly, it has been argued that the best way to overcome this is to provide the child with an experience of reading, it also seems clear that young children benefit by being given a period of intensive word-recognition work.

It seems from my experience that the most efficient way to teach children common high-frequency words (especially those not pronounced how they would commonly be sounded) is to give them frequent opportunities to read such words, either in context or in isolation. Obviously, much of this work should involve the use of words in context.

In summary:
• While it is accepted that reading should involve a search for meaning, this process requires the efficient sampling of visual information. The instant

recognition of commonly occurring words aids this search for meaning.

• You should attempt to develop basic word recognition using one of the commonly used sight-word lists. The Johnson list (Johnson 1971) is possibly the most useful one available.

• While these words should first be introduced in context, at times frequent opportunities to read these words in isolation will help the development of basic sight-word knowledge. An approach combining work on words in context, so that children more fully understand the meaning of the words (as well as their syntactic function), and some work with words in isolation, seems to be the most efficient way rapidly to increase sight-word knowledge.

As a final point, while undoubtedly *it is the author's message that should be the essential focus, rather than the author's words*, you should not forget that the instant recognition of some of these words usually makes it easier to understand the message the author is conveying.

The following activities are simple ideas I have found useful for developing word recognition skills.

SKILLS	ACTIVITIES
• Recognising own names in print	✪ Give all children name tags. ✪ Place names on desks, clothes, books, etc. ✪ Ask children to bring photographs of themselves to school. Place their names underneath, and create a wall chart.
• Recognising meaningful captions, labels or sentences (related to own experience)	✪ Make up interesting sentence labels, based on children's experiences, to place around the classroom (e.g. *Giraffes please duck*, over the door following the reading of *Never Talk to Strangers*; *This machine eats pencils*, next to the pencil sharpener; *Fingers will be eaten*, on the goldfish tank; *John's five today*, next to John).
• Matching a label/phrase with another label/phrase	✪ Provide children with phrase flashcards to play Snap with. ✪ Ask children to match a phrase or label on a card with another placed next to an object in the room. ✪ Have two teams, each member of the team holding a phrase card that matches a card held by the other team. Children (one at a time) attempt to match their cards with those of the other team.
• Matching a word with a word and picture	✪ Provide children with word flashcards to match with corresponding word-and-picture cards.
• Matching a word with a picture	✪ This time require children to match word cards with corresponding picture cards.

- Reading own captions (scribed by teacher)

✪ Ask children to think of appropriate captions for objects, artwork, science work, and the like. At a later time, ask them to read their own captions.

- Reading own experience stories (scribed by teacher)

✪ Ask children to read their own stories. These may be their observations, feelings, memories, etc.

- Reading experience stories of others

✪ Publish children's stories, so that they can share each other's work.

- Recognising environmental words

✪ Use words within children's environment as starting points for the development of sight words. Children will know many words when they arrive at school; share these with other children (e.g. *Stop, Woolworths, No Smoking, Walk*).

✪ Present known environmental words in different type forms (e.g. *STOP, stop, Stop*).

✪ Use home and family words. These will usually be of great interest to children (e.g. *mum, dad, sister, dog, house*).

At this stage, most children are ready to learn a large number of words rapidly. While the following skills are arranged in sequence, in most classrooms they will be introduced and reinforced simultaneously.

SKILLS

ACTIVITIES

- Recognising action words

✪ Produce an 'I can ...' book for class reading. Ask each child to suggest a verb (e.g. *skip, jump, climb*) for you to scribe and him/her to illustrate.

- Recognising common nouns

✪ Ideally, select words children are interested in. Ask them to suggest words (e.g. *motorbike, car, truck, spaceship, football*).
✪ Make a 'Words we know' chart.
✪ Make a class thesaurus (children illustrate).
✪ Create a wall mural.
✪ Produce a class book on special topics (e.g. 'Things I like').

- Recognising structural words (e.g. *I'm, this, my*)

✪ Produce class caption books with consistent sentence patterns (e.g. *This is ..., I can ..., I like ...*).

- Recognising colour words

✪ Make a colour chart.
✪ Produce a class colour book. Have children cut pictures of specific colours out of a magazine; ask them to suggest captions (e.g. *two green racing cars, green trees*).

• Recognising number words

⊛ Produce class number books, using a similar approach to the above. A book on the number 3 would lead to captions like *three fat cats* and *three fast cars*.

• Recognising days of the week

⊛ Have a class date and weather board for completion each day.

At this stage in their development, most children will be starting to read many simple books, and success is essential. If you support a basal approach as part of your reading program, devote part of the introduction (to any story) to an examination of new sight words.

Other teachers have found it useful also to spend some time each week introducing words from a common sight-word list (e.g. the Johnson list [Johnson 1971]). These words are dealt with because of the frequency with which they occur in children's reading material.

A common approach used to introduce new words is as follows:

Step 1   Print the word on the board, on a flashcard, or under a picture.

Step 2   Read the word, and relate it, if possible, to children's experience.

Step 3   Ask children to use the word in a sentence. Have the class think of synonyms for the word.

Step 4   Discuss a possible meaning of the word. If appropriate, use the word in different contexts, and examine the way the meaning changes.

Step 5   This step is optional, but it is sometimes necessary for certain children. Ask children to copy (or trace) the word. Some children may keep a personal dictionary.

The above procedure need not be followed for every word or every child. However, it will probably prove quite useful for some beginning readers or for older children who have experienced reading problems. The following further ideas and activities sometimes prove useful:

Word banks   Each time a child learns a new word, deposit it in the 'bank'. This may be either a workbook or a card system.

Word hunts   Ask children to search a story for a special word and perhaps to check to see how many times it occurs.

Card games   A wide range of card games can be played, most requiring nothing more than small cards with appropriate words written on them (usually in multiples of two). Old favourites are Snap and Concentration. Concentration is also a good memory game. Place all cards face down in a grid pattern. Players (two to four) take turns turning over two cards at a time. The object of the game is to find pairs. If a pair is found, the player keeps them; if not, the cards are turned face down again.

Board games   These are best played in pairs. Many traditional games can be used in this way (e.g. Snakes and Ladders, Ludo, Monopoly)—in fact, any game requiring dice. Simply replace the dice with flashcards, each having a small number (1–6) in the top right-hand corner. Players turn a card over, say the word, then count the number of spaces indicated by the number in the corner.

Group participation games   Many games are suitable for small groups (or even whole classes at times). Some of the many games I have used include:

✸ *Buried treasure*   Simply place a set of four to eight cards along the board ledge, and ask a child to hide the 'treasure' behind one card while other children hide their heads (a simple cross on the board will do for the treasure). Children take turns attempting to find the treasure: 'Is it hidden behind …?'

✸ *Drop the card*   Play this exactly like Drop the Hanky, substituting a flashcard for the handkerchief.

✸ *Hopscotch*   Write words or place flashcards in the squares. Children call out words as they hop through.

✸ *Station game*   Flash 4 to 10 words at the group. Children who identify words keep them before finally coming out to the front of the class. Other group members take turns moving from station to station saying the words.

✸ *Human 0's and X's*   Play this game with two teams. Team members have turns identifying words. If correct they go to the front of the room to take part in the 0's and X's (have a large grid on the floor). Play the game just like normal 0's and X's. One team kneels while the other stands up.

Blackboard races   These games are simple, effective and are lots of fun. There are many variations on the racing theme, e.g. Space Race, Grand Prix, The Olympics.

To play each of these games, simply draw the game on the board with clear divisions (e.g. a series of planets). Teams jump from segment to segment as they identify words correctly. Differentiate between teams by using different colours.

A note concerning games:

Games can be quite useful as long as they are not overused. They have the obvious advantage that they are a fun way to consolidate sight words. However, when using any game, ask yourself the following questions:

• Do children have frequent opportunities to respond?
• Does the game require children to learn complex rules before playing it?
• Does the game require a great deal of teacher preparation?

If the answer is 'No' to any of these questions, try something else.

Phonic analysis

Probably no single aspect of reading instruction has created more disagreement than **phonics**. There has even been disagreement about the name. Do we call it phonics? Word attack? Decoding skills? Some have even incorrectly labelled it 'phonetics'.

There is obviously universal agreement that a knowledge of sound–symbol relationships is of some use in reading. However, there is wide disagreement concerning the degree of importance of this knowledge for readers, and the place of phonics instruction in any reading program.

On one side, some teachers and researchers suggest that all children must learn sound–symbol relationships before commencing reading; while on the other side, there are those who argue that formal instruction has no place. The latter argue that, because of the great inconsistency in the relationship between sound and symbols in our language, formal instruction is pointless; the only way for children to acquire phonic knowledge is by reading.

Advocates of phonic programs for readers have usually used one or more of the following approaches.

Synthetic approach

This approach involves the systematic teaching of letter–sound correspondences. Even within this approach, great diversity exists. Some teachers begin by teaching a child all the vowels, followed by the consonants; these are then combined to form v-c words. Other teachers start by teaching several consonants before introducing the vowels; once again, these sounds are combined to form words. A further approach (commonly termed the 'Hay-Wingo' approach) involves teaching consonant–vowel combinations first, which are then blended with a consonant (e.g. *ca-t*, *cat*).

While there is variation in the above approaches, all possess the main characteristics of **synthetic** approaches: they involve the systematic teaching of specific sounds, which the child is then taught to blend to form words.

My experience with children has shown that this approach, which views early reading as something that should be learnt from part to whole only, has many weaknesses. The most obvious weakness is that it teaches children that reading involves the exact detailed sequential perception and identification of letters and sounds. Clearly, real reading does not simply involve this. Children taught to read using a purely synthetic approach fail to grasp that reading involves primarily a search for meaning, which requires the use of many *different* strategies.

Synthetic approaches probably have a place in the reading program for specific children who do not respond to other approaches. However, there seems little justification for their widespread use in classrooms.

Rule approach

This approach is based upon the premise that some phonic generalisations are reliable enough to allow the formation of specific rules that help the child to decode words. Some of the most common rules are:
• Any time a vowel is followed by two identical consonants, it is short (e.g. *clapped*).
• The letter *c* is pronounced *s* before *e*, *i* and *y*, but pronounced *k* otherwise.
• When two vowels go a-walking, the first one does the talking (e.g. *boat*).
• When a word ends with a silent *e*, it makes the preceding vowel say its name (e.g. *pipe*).

The problems with this approach are obvious. First, it is difficult to find any rule that is always correct. For example, what about the pronunciation of *rough*, *'cello*, *questionnaire* and *crepe*? Clearly, the above rules do not apply.

Further, even though the rules may be right some of the time, there seems little justification for using any approach to reading that requires the reader to recite a rule before decoding a single sound within a single word. Any reader using such techniques is not reading for meaning.

In my opinion, this approach is of little use and should be avoided.

Phonic family approach

This approach is similar to the synthetic approach, because it stresses the learning of specific **phonograms**, which are then blended with consonants to form words.

It still stresses the learning of reading from part to whole, but the 'parts' are larger (e.g. *c-at*, *cat*; *r-ing*, *ring*). While it suffers from the same weaknesses as the synthetic methods, it is sometimes useful for young readers, to make them aware that words are composed of separate sounds blended together. It has the advantage that it does not require (or encourage) the child to break a word into single letter sounds. It tends to encourage the child to sample chunks of words in search of meaning, rather than sounding everything out.

Analytic approach

The **analytic** approach attempts to heighten children's awareness of sound–symbol relationships, by pointing out consistencies (and inconsistencies) within words they have learnt as sight words.

Sometimes with this approach, children are provided with reading material with specific phonic units used consistently. Reading such material presumably reinforces their knowledge of sound–symbol relationships, which can then be used in other reading situations.

This method obviously stresses the teaching of reading from whole to part. It has the advantage that it allows the child to gain a knowledge of both the consistencies and the inconsistencies of sound–symbol relationships, within the context of real reading.

A final word on phonics

In spite of the constant controversy surrounding the place of phonics in the reading program, there can be little doubt that proficient readers obviously require some phonic knowledge for efficient reading. However, when teaching reading you should remember the following points:

• Reading requires the use of much more than phonic knowledge to enable meaning to be extracted from print.

• Over-reliance on phonic methods (especially synthetic approaches) may have a detrimental effect on a child's ability to read for meaning.

• Phonic knowledge is often best developed by providing children with frequent opportunities to read; that is, it is predominantly 'caught not taught'.

• Children who lack phonic knowledge should be given help, using methods that stress the development of this knowledge within real reading.

• Children do not learn sound–symbol relationships in a definite order, although experienced teachers frequently observe that certain phonic units are acquired more easily than others.

• Phonic instruction is not necessary before children commence real reading; in fact, this should generally be avoided.

The above discussion should make it perfectly clear that I find little justification for providing all children with systematic phonic instruction. However, there will always be a small number of children who do require instruction in some form to increase their knowledge of sound–symbol relationships. Experienced teachers have found that these children tend to find certain phonic units easier to learn than others. As a result, I include below a sequence that, I have found, approximates the natural growth that occurs in many 'typical' readers. Obviously, no two readers will ever acquire phonic knowledge in exactly the same sequence. However, this sequence, and the activities that accompany it, may be useful when you are working with specific children requiring phonic instruction.

SKILLS	ACTIVITIES
• Matching an initial consonant sound (presented orally) with an object	✪ Present objects, name them, and say: 'What sound does this start with?' ✪ Ask children to think of something that begins with a specific sound (e.g. 'Who can think of a boy's name starting with p [sound]?'). ✪ Play I Spy (e.g. 'I spy with my little eye something beginning with t [sound]').
• Recognising and recalling: * consonants (e.g. *s, m, f, t, l, g, b, c*); * short vowels; * other consonants (e.g.	✪ As mentioned above, any teaching of phonics should occur as much as possible as part of real reading. While isolated words will be used from time to time, they should have a clear meaning. A general approach I have found useful involves the following steps:

n, p, h, r, w, d, j, k, y, z, -x, qu);
* association between lower and upper case letters;
* simple word families, i.e. v-c blending (e.g. *at, in, it, up, on, am, an, us*);
* other word families (e.g. *ug, op, un, ig, ix*);
* three-letter word families (e.g. *ing*);
* simple consonant digraphs (e.g. *sh, th, ck, wh*);
* initial consonant blends (e.g. *tr, dr, gr, cr, st, bl, fr, fl, gl, pl, pr*);
* final consonant blends (e.g. *nd, st, mp, nt, nk, ft, ld, lt*);
* simple vowel digraphs and diphthongs (e.g. *ee, oo, ay, ar*);
* long vowel *y* as in *my*;
* long vowels;
* three-letter initial-consonant blends (e.g. *str, spr, shr, thr, squ*);
* short vowel *y* as in *baby*;
* other digraphs and diphthongs (e.g. *oy, er, oa, ai, or, ar, ou, ow, ea, ur, ay, ir, aw, oi, ew, ie, ui, ph*);
* two sounds each of *c* and *g*;
* silent letters (e.g. *knee*); and
* other phonograms (e.g. *augh, ough, aught, ought, eight, our*)

Step 1 Once children have learnt a number of words (using look–say techniques and language experience), get them to look for consistencies and inconsistencies in the words they know. From simple books or language experience stories, they can perhaps write three or four words that have something in common (e.g. *Helen, hops, her, happily*).

Step 2 Ask children to read each word aloud, paying special attention to its beginning, middle and end sounds. Ask: 'Do the words start or end the same way?', 'What have they in common?'

Step 3 Next ask children to think of other words that have the same beginning, end or medial sound. Add these words to the words you started with, and place them on the board. Words that have the same sound but different spellings should be placed in a separate list.

Step 4 Ask children to read the list again. Discuss each word's meaning, and use it in oral sentences (several, if it can have different meanings). Write the words in personal dictionaries (if these are used).

Step 5 Finally, compose some sentences together, and write them on the board. Perhaps children can make up some sentences of their own.

Do not overuse this technique. Use it only when children have failed to acquire sufficient phonic knowledge through real reading. This advice also applies to the following activities:

✪ **Sound lotto** Call out (or appoint a group leader to call out) words with sounds that correspond to lists children have. Each child is required to circle a word that is similar (e.g. same starting, end or middle sound).

✪ **Word detective** Give children a short passage, and ask them quickly to search for and circle as many words as they can that have specific beginning, end or middle sounds.

✪ **Matching activities** There are many variations of matching activity. At its simplest level, it involves matching an initial sound with a phonic family (e.g. *p-ot*). The use of word wheels, flip cards and string cards all involves the same principle. They have some *limited* usefulness for children who lack phonic knowledge and who find it difficult to attack a new word.

⊛ **Beanbag game** Draw a grid on a large sheet of cardboard, and write specific sounds in each square (e.g. *dr*, *pr*, *tr*). Children take turns throwing the beanbag and must think of a word that includes the sound they land on.

⊛ **Phonic dice** Children roll two or three dice (large foam or polystyrene) that have specific sounds on each face, then blend the sounds to form words.

⊛ **Snap** Include words with similar beginning, middle and final sounds. Children 'snap' when two cards with a similar sound are turned up.

⊛ **Board games** Many traditional board games can be used (e.g. Snakes and Ladders) by substituting for dice sound–word cards with a number from 1 to 6 written in the top right-hand corner. Each child turns a word up, sounds and says it, then counts the spaces indicated by the number.

⊛ **Phonic cloze activities** Omit initial, final or medial sounds, instead of deleting the whole word. Then encourage children to use limited phonic knowledge (as well as semantic and syntactic information) to predict the word.

⊛ **Word concentration** Play this like ordinary Concentration, except that children have to match words with similar sounds.

Structural analysis

While the teaching of phonics is based upon **phonemes**, which are the smallest units of sound in our language (roughly forty-five in number), structural analysis is concerned with the teaching of **morphemes**, which are the smallest units of meaning.

Our language is made up of thousands of morphemes. Some words contain only one, but others are made up of several (e.g. *sun,* a single morpheme; *sunshine,* two morphemes).

Many teachers have used the principles of structural analysis in the form of word-building exercises (e.g. *thick, thicker, thickest*).

One advantage of structural analysis over phonic analysis is that it is meaning based. However, as with phonics, there seems little point in exposing every child to a structured program that aims to teach children specific morphemes. Obviously, a working knowledge of common morphemes is a valuable aid for readers when encountering unknown words, but it should be remembered that using one's knowledge of specific morphemes (like phonic knowledge) is only one of the many strategies used in reading, and a strategy that will usually be learnt when children are provided with frequent opportunities to read. There are so many morphemes that a structured approach to the development of this knowledge is pointless. It should also be remembered that it is misleading to teach some morphemes in isolation anyway, because of their inconsistency (e.g. in *untold* and *untie*, the prefix *un* has a different meaning in each word).

However, some specific structural components do occur so frequently in our language that sometimes it is useful (and at times desirable) to help children to discover them as part of real reading.

The following is an attempt to outline some of the more common morphemes and activities that help to develop a knowledge of them.

SKILLS

- Recognising simple endings:
  * plural *s* (e.g. *cars*)
  * *ing* (e.g. *playing*)
  * *ed* (e.g. *jumped*)
  * *er* (e.g. *driver*)
  * *ies* (e.g. *babies*)
  * *ly* (e.g. *lovely*)
- Understanding comparative forms of words (e.g. *fast, faster, fastest*)
- Recognising and understanding compound words (e.g. *bedroom*)
- Recognising and understanding simple contractions (e.g. *I'm, I am*)
- Recognising simple prefixes and suffixes (e.g. *be, sub, ment*)

ACTIVITIES

✪ **Analytic approaches** The following activities are probably the most effective way to increase a child's knowledge of these structural analysis components:

Word search Ask children to quickly scan a page and to underline words with a specific morpheme.

Morpheme build-up Write several words with a common morpheme on the board. Discuss the morpheme included, and ask children to think of other similar words. Add them to the list. Ask children to read them, use them in sentences, and add them to a personal dictionary.

Compound word breakdown Examine specific compound words, and break them into root words and morphemes. This can be extended to examine the different structural composition of certain compound words.

Word quizzes Ask children questions like: 'What would you call a car driver who races?' or the reverse, 'If a fisherman is a man who fishes, what would you call a salesman?'

Cloze exercises Produce cloze exercises with some of the root words left in (or with the root word missing). The child adds another morpheme to complete the word.

Synthetic activities These are of limited use, but with specific children they may be useful (e.g. flip cards, consisting of root words on one card and affixes on another; compound word dominoes; compound word jigsaws).

Durkin approach Dolores Durkin (1972) has suggested a combined synthetic–analytic approach. This involves the step-by-step dismantling of a word and its reassembly (e.g. *helplessness, helpless, help, helpless, helplessness*).

CHAPTER FOUR
Comprehension

Comprehension describes our ability to recall, understand and interpret a message communicated in any form. Such a definition assumes that the recall, understanding and interpretation of a written, spoken or visual message are essentially the same. That is, similar processing skills are used whether we are listening, reading or observing.

Reading, like any form of communication, is primarily seen as a thinking process. While a reader cannot read without sampling visual data from a page of print, an author's message can only be understood if the reader is actively involved in a search for meaning.

As outlined in Chapter 1, research indicates that the ability to comprehend the author's message depends upon many factors, including the reader's:
- knowledge of the content of the reading material;
- understanding of the structure of language;
- ability to concentrate on the author's message;
- knowledge of the meanings of words;
- purpose for reading; and
- understanding of the reading process.

The above definition of reading comprehension and the factors that influence it entails a number of clear implications for the teaching of comprehension:

Identification of comprehension skills Comprehension *cannot* be thought of as a set of separate but loosely connected subskills. You cannot teach comprehension by introducing a series of isolated subskills in the hope that the reader will then 'bring it all together'.

However, this does not mean that we cannot identify definite skills, which can be practised. This can be done, but the manner in which this practice is carried out is very important. It should not occur as a series of isolated formal exercises in a carefully structured sequence. Rather, it should occur in response to a child's need, and within the context of real reading.

Development of written comprehension ability This can be fostered through activities designed to stimulate the comprehension of spoken and visual messages.

This is extremely important for the young or failing reader; the opportunity to apply higher comprehension skills to spoken and visual stimuli is valuable preparatory work for reading comprehension. In fact, one of the most effective ways to stimulate comprehension ability is to provide a classroom environment in which children are constantly asked (and are encouraged to ask themselves) 'Why?', 'How?' and 'What if ...?'

Comprehension teaching involves far more than just providing a silent reading passage followed by a set of written questions.

Comprehension skills taxonomy   A useful way to ensure that you question children at a variety of levels is by familiarising yourself with a comprehension skills taxonomy. While there are many taxonomies, which often disagree, it is probably useful to be aware of some of the broad categories outlined within them. In this way you are constantly reminded that it is important to question beyond the literal level.

A useful taxonomy is that suggested by Nila Banton Smith (1970), which consists of four broad levels:

• *Literal comprehension questions*   At this level the question is concerned with the direct literal recall of a word, sentence or idea (e.g. recalling details, recognising character traits, recognising a sequence).

• *Interpretive comprehension questions*   At this level the reader has to supply meaning that is not stated directly in the text; he/she has to read 'between the lines' (e.g. reasoning cause and effect, anticipating outcomes, making generalisations).

• *Critical comprehension questions*   At this level the reader is required to evaluate and pass judgement on the quality, accuracy, value or truthfulness of what is read (e.g. identifying the author's bias, detecting propaganda).

• *Creative comprehension questions*   At this level the reader needs to go beyond the author's text, to express new ideas, solve a problem or gain new insights; the reader must read 'beyond the lines' (e.g. responding emotionally, suggesting alternative solutions to a problem raised).

To illustrate each of these question types further, here is an example at each level. All the questions relate to the story *The Pied Piper*:

• What job did the townspeople ask the Piper to do? (literal)

• Do you think that the townspeople would ever try to trick another person? Why? or Why not? (interpretive)

• Should the Piper have taken all the children away? Why? or Why not? (critical)

• How might the townspeople have removed the rats without the Piper's help? (creative)

A knowledge of a taxonomy like the above is obviously useful for classroom teachers. A conscious effort should be made to provide children with a good balance of all these questions.

Choice of reading material   The material that children read has an important effect upon their ability to comprehend. You should avoid using reading material with a heavily stilted or artificial sentence or story structure. Initially, you should also avoid material that has content well outside children's actual experiences.

This is particularly important with the beginning and failing reader. The initial use of a language experience approach with these children is obviously one of the easiest ways to overcome this problem. Such an approach allows the beginning reader to use his/her own knowledge of context and understanding of language to extract meaning from the print.

Reading–language integration Reading should be integrated as much as possible with all aspects of language. If children are reading about something they have also talked about, written about, heard about and drawn, they are in a much better position to understand the written message, because they bring much more information to the reading situation. That is, it becomes easier for reading to take the form of an active thinking process.

Expansion of written vocabulary Because of the importance to reading comprehension of understanding word meanings, frequent opportunities should be provided for all children to expand their written vocabulary.

Knowledge of language structure A reader's understanding and knowledge of the structure of language at both sentence and story level is also very important for reading comprehension. Perhaps the most effective way to further this knowledge is by reading good literature to children (preferably daily) and by providing a similar variety of quality literature for children to read.

In summary then, you can do a number of things to encourage the development of each child's comprehension ability:

• Base early reading upon the language and experience of the child.

• Provide opportunities for children to read daily from a wide range of material that interests them.
• Provide instruction that aims to improve reading comprehension only as part of real reading.
• Adopt an approach to teaching, in all areas of the school curriculum, that has as a central component the use of questioning at the literal, interpretive, critical and creative levels. Above all, create a classroom environment that encourages children to question and reflect upon their own observations, by asking themselves questions like: 'Why is that so?', 'Can I prove it?', 'How did it occur?', 'What will happen next?'
• Provide frequent opportunities for oral comprehension development, and recognise that this is valuable preparation for written comprehension.
• Remember that reading comprehension should involve far more than a passage followed by ten questions, a series of basal workbooks or an intensive period using a reading laboratory.

You should not assume from the above discussion that it is not possible to isolate specific comprehension skills for instruction. This can and should be done. One of the greatest mistakes you can make is to assume that simply allowing children to read daily is sufficient to permit the development of all comprehension skills. Children need your *help*, especially in relation to comprehension at the critical and creative levels.

Often this help will simply involve asking the child a variety of questions while you are reading a story or after the reading. At other times, you may simply ask children to evaluate critically the content of a story through small group discussion. Sometimes, give work in one specific area of comprehension (e.g. detecting an author's bias, making judgements relating to the logic of an author's argument).

An attempt is made on the following pages to outline a number of important comprehension skills. This outline is included to make you more aware of the variety of skills that can be developed. You should remember that virtually any comprehensive skill can be dealt with by children at any stage of reading development. However, some specific activities are more appropriate for children at different stages of development. As a result, the skills and activities given are grouped for readers at specific stages of development.

The activities that accompany each skill are not designed to be used for isolated skills practice. Rather, they are included to illustrate how the development of each skill can be encouraged in response to pupil need at various levels within the context of an integrated language program. Perhaps an example of the type of approach I have used will help to clarify how this can be done.

A sample comprehension lesson

The ability to summarise is an example of a skill that is very rarely acquired naturally and that frequently causes problems. Many children, even at ten to twelve years of age, often simply copy 'slabs' of material from a book when asked to take notes. How should this skill be developed? What is your role in its development? Certainly, it should not be tackled through a series of isolated exercises.

Having observed that instruction on summarising is needed, give a series of lessons. The first lesson may arise quite spontaneously, while you are observing a child or group working on a special research assignment. Plan further lessons probably at specific intervals. The lessons may proceed (remember, there is never only one approach) in the following manner:

Step 1   Tell children: 'I'm going to read this section from Greg's book on whales. I want you to listen to it, so that you can tell me what it is mainly about [the topic], as well as being able to tell me some of the most important things it says about the topic.' In other words, give them a purpose for listening and comprehending.

Step 2   Read the extract.

Step 3   Ask: 'Who can tell me the topic of the extract I've just read?' In effect, ask children to find the main ideas. When they respond, place all topics suggested on the board. Then, following a brief discussion, select one as the most appropriate topic.

Step 4   Say: 'Quickly think of all the things you can remember that tell us about this main topic.' That is, ask children simply to recall details. Record all contributions on the board.

Step 5   Say: 'Let's look to see if we have repeated any points. Can we cross any out?' As children respond, make amendments to the list.

Step 6   Ask: 'Are these points all equally important? Can we leave some out?' In other words, ask children to find significant details. Cross out less important details as they respond.

Step 7   Ask: 'Are these points in the best order, or should we change them around?' That is, ask children to sequence ideas and prepare an outline of the extract. As they respond, number the relevant points in order.

Step 8   Specific children may then attempt to turn this outline into their own summary. However, you may well save this step until later lessons.

This is only one lesson in a sequence of lessons designed to lead ultimately to the stage where the child can select a book, read an extract, then prepare his/her own summary. The lesson itself illustrates many of the principles discussed above:

• It is designed to develop one skill, but it clearly involves the use of a number of skills within the same lesson.

• It is the first lesson in a sequence, and hence shows how the ultimate skill to be developed can be attempted at different levels of difficulty. In this case, all work is oral.

• It is conducted in response to a perceived need.

Obviously, the secret of success with such an approach is, first, know your children, and secondly, be aware of some of the many comprehension skills that are important for reading.

All the skills and activities outlined below are grouped, for convenience, into four developmental stages, so that the activities suggested are appropriate for children at different stages of development.

Stage 1: Beginning reading

(5.0 to 6.0 years approx.)

At this beginning stage of the child's development, it has often been assumed that comprehension development is irrelevant. However, this is certainly not the case. Well before children learn to read, they can comprehend; effective communication depends upon it. Your main responsibility at this stage of the child's development is to stimulate oral comprehension ability. This is best achieved through incidental treatment. The following activities are included as examples of the many ways in which you can foster this development within the context of real language experiences.

SKILLS	ACTIVITIES
Oral comprehension	
• Sequencing events	✪ Ask children to put a series of very simple pictures (two to five) into sequence. Initially, two or three pictures will suffice. Photographs are ideal for this purpose (especially if based on children's experience). As an extension, children will enjoy dictating captions for each photograph, to form a simple story. ✪ Ask children to put into sequence pictures that correspond to a story you have read to them. ✪ Ask children to draw a series of pictures that depict the key events in a story. ✪ Read nursery rhymes or television jingles. Write out a common rhyme or jingle, then cut it into separate lines. Ask children to place the lines in the correct sequence. Selected children can read each line.
• Finding the main idea	✪ After reading a story, ask children to suggest a suitable title. ✪ Ask children to suggest a title for a picture they have examined. ✪ After reading a story, show children several pictures, and ask them to select the picture that best depicts the main idea of the story.
• Recalling significant details	✪ After reading a story, ask children to outline the main events in it. ✪ Ask children to select important details from a picture.
• Classifying information	✪ On the board, list all the children's observations about a picture (e.g. names of all the

animals they can see in the picture). Then ask children to suggest ways in which the information can be grouped or classified (e.g. by number of legs, by size).

• Seeing relationships between events

✪ Discuss relationships between events in a picture (e.g. 'Why did this boy fall off his bike?', 'Why do you think he was riding it there?').

✪ Discuss the events in a story you have read to children, asking questions relating to specific incidents (e.g. 'Why do you think the water kept getting higher while the fox was carrying the Gingerbread Man across the river?').

• Dramatising stories heard

✪ Select children to play all the characters in a story (e.g. *Are You My Mother?*).

• Reasoning: Why? How? When?

✪ Following (and during) a film, story, television program or first-hand experience, ask children questions that make them reason why, how or when (e.g. 'Why does popcorn pop?', 'Why do fish have gills?', 'Why might the Pied Piper's music have attracted the children?', 'How could the Gingerbread Man have escaped from the fox?').

• Anticipating outcomes

✪ Stop midway through a story to ask: 'How may this story end?', 'What will happen to . . .?'

• Distinguishing between real and imaginary stories and events

✪ After reading a story, ask: 'Could this story really have happened?'

✪ Ask specific questions relating to a picture, film or story (e.g. 'Do you think a forest really grew in Max's bedroom?' [*Where the Wild Things Are*]).

• Making comparisons

✪ Compare events or characters in stories, daily

events and pictures (e.g. 'Look at these two pictures. Is it the same time of the day?', 'How can you tell?').

• Determining character traits

✪ Ask children to offer opinions of characters in a story (e.g. 'Was Grandma a kind person?', 'Do you like Connie?', 'Why?' [*The Folk of the Faraway Tree*]).

Stage 2: Early reading development

(6.0 to 8.0 years approx.)

At this stage children make rapid reading progress but your main responsibility is still to stimulate oral comprehension ability. Many higher-order comprehension skills, which traditionally have been 'saved up' until later primary grades, can be dealt with through oral activities at this stage.

However, whereas most of the previous work has been concerned with comprehension of aurally and visually presented material, at this stage you should give children greater opportunities to discuss material they have read themselves. The use of written activities should be kept to a minimum.

SKILLS

ACTIVITIES

Oral comprehension

• Sequencing events

✪ Read a short extract to children, then present separate sentences (starting with two) and ask children to place them in the correct order.

✪ Get children to discuss a series of pictures and place them in correct sequence. Cartoons are excellent for this purpose.

• Finding the main idea

✪ Read short extracts to children, and ask them to suggest the main idea (or topic) of each piece. As a variation, ask them to depict the main idea of a drawing.

✪ Show children single frame cartoons, and ask them to suggest a suitable caption.

• Recalling significant details

✪ After reading a short extract, ask children to suggest the topic of the piece and the important details that 'tell us about the topic'.

✪ Following a film or television program, ask children to outline the important events. Perhaps list them on the board.

✪ Following an excursion or first-hand experience (e.g. cooking), ask a small group to record the main events using pictures. Collate the pictures in sequence, to form a book.

- Classifying information

✪ After reading a short extract, ask children to list a number of important points and then classify them. For example, after reading *The Bear Detectives,* have children list all the clues the bears found and (separately) all the mistakes Pop made.

- Seeing relationships between events

✪ After (or while) reading a story, ask children questions concerning the relationship between characters or events (e.g. 'Why do you think the animals wanted Max to be King?', 'Do you think Max would have been glad to be back home?', 'Why?' [*Where the Wild Things Are*]).

- Dramatising stories read

✪ Select a group to dramatise a segment from a story (e.g. the scene inside the classroom when Piper Paw starts to misbehave [*No Kiss for Mother*]).

✪ Select two children to repeat a dialogue between two characters in a story (e.g. the lighthouse keeper and his wife discussing how to trick the seagulls [*The Lighthouse Keeper's Lunch*]).

- Reasoning: Why? How? When?

✪ During (or following) a story, film, television program, science experiment or picture talk, ask children questions that require more than simple observation or factual reporting. These questions should be open-ended, so that all children are able to offer a response (e.g. 'What other methods might the lighthouse keeper, in *The Lighthouse Keeper's Lunch*, have used to trick the seagulls?', 'Why do sunflowers turn their heads during the day?', 'How might Jack have stopped the giant from following him without cutting down the beanstalk?').

✪ **Twenty questions** Have one child think of an object, person or event, and allow other children twenty questions to find out what it is. The questions are simply answered with 'Yes' or 'No'.

- Anticipating outcomes

✪ Ask children to predict the ending for a story, before you reach it.

✪ Ask children to predict what a story is about, simply from the title.

- Distinguishing between real and imaginary stories and events

✪ Ask specific questions relating to a picture, film, television show or story (e.g. 'Could a frog really drink a lake?' [*What Made Tiddalik Laugh?*]).

- Making a judgement concerning story context

⊛ During (or following) a story, ask questions that require children to make value judgements (e.g. 'Should Goldilocks have entered the three bears' house?', 'Should Jack have swapped the cow for the magic beans?').

⊛ Discuss moral dilemma stories (e.g. 'What should . . . do?').

- Detecting mood

⊛ After reading a story, ask children about their feelings (e.g. 'How does the story make you feel?', 'How does the action of the Pied Piper make you feel?', 'Do you think the writer wanted you to feel that way?').

- Making comparisons

⊛ Comparing events or characters in stories, daily events and pictures (e.g. 'Does . . . seem older than his sister in the story?').

- Determining character traits

⊛ Ask children to offer opinions of characters in stories, poems, films and television shows (e.g. 'Tell me what you think of Max' [*Where the Wild Things Are*]). List ideas on the board.

Written comprehension

- Recalling details from a story

⊛ Have children read a story then answer simple literal questions about it (e.g. 'How old was . . .?', 'Whom did . . . chase?').

⊛ **Sentence matching** Ask children to match the beginnings and endings of events from a story.

- Determining the main idea

⊛ Ask children to draw a picture to show what a story was mainly about.

⊛ Show children a series of sentences relating to a story they have read, and ask them which is closest to the main idea.

⊛ Ask children to write appropriate captions for pictures or single frame cartoons.

- Determining character traits

⊛ Have children read a story then tick words or sentences that describe one of the characters.

⊛ Ask children to match descriptive statements with the names of characters in a story.

Stage 3: Growth in reading

(8.0 to 10.0 years approx.)

At this stage of their development, children make rapid progress in comprehension. They start to find the interpretation of their own reading much easier and are able critically to analyse both aurally and visually presented material.

Your main responsibility at this stage is to stimulate the child's desire to read 'between' and 'beyond' the lines. This will involve a great deal of discussion (small group, individual or class) concerning material children have read themselves. The place of written activities will start to become more important as a valuable means for evaluating individual responses. However, these activities *must* not become purely methods for *testing* comprehension. Rather, they should be used to further each child's understanding of reading as a thinking process.

SKILLS	ACTIVITIES

Oral comprehension

* Finding the main idea

✪ Ask children to suggest the main idea (topic sentence) for specific paragraphs in a story.

* Recalling significant details

✪ Following a story, film or television program, ask children to suggest all the important details they can remember. List these details on the board, then examine them to see if they are equally important.

* Classifying information

✪ Following a story, film, television program or first-hand experience, ask children to suggest important ideas or observations, then classify them. For example, after a nature ramble, ask children to recall all their important observations. List these observations on the board, then attempt to classify them into categories.

* Dramatising stories read

✪ Select several children or a large group to dramatise a section of a story (or the entire story). Children may:
  * dramatise their favourite part of the story;
  * conduct an interview with a character from the story;
  * prepare a dialogue between two characters in the story; or
  * dramatise the whole story.

* Reasoning: Why? How? When?

✪ During (or following) a story, film, television program or science experiment, ask children questions that go beyond simple observation or reporting (e.g. 'Why did Charlotte like Wilbur?', 'How might Charlotte have saved Wilbur, though she couldn't write and spell?' [*Charlotte's Web*]).

✪ **Bag game** Place in a bag a set of four or five objects that are related in some way (e.g. billy-can, newspaper advertisement, camping gear, shopping list, note with details of a meeting, map). Ask a group of four or five children to examine the note, discuss the relationship between the objects, and then compose an oral story that they must retell (each taking a part).

• Anticipating outcomes

★ Ask children to predict the end of a story before reaching it.

★ Ask children to suggest what a story may be about purely from the title, or what a newspaper article is about simply from the headline.

★ Show children a cartoon strip with the last frame missing (use an overhead projector). Ask them to suggest how it may end. Perhaps get them to draw the last frame.

• Distinguishing between real and imaginary stories and events

★ Ask children to suggest parts that could be real and parts that could be imaginary from a story, film or television show. For example, after reading *The Super Roo of Mungalongaloo*, ask children to suggest the events that were imaginary.

★ Present a story on an overhead projector, and underline the parts of it that could not happen in real life.

• Making a judgement concerning story content

★ During (or following) a story, ask questions that require children to make a value judgement (e.g. 'Should people kill animals for food?', 'Is it fair to prepare animals for shows?' [*Charlotte's Web*]).

★ Discuss controversial issues (e.g. 'Should men kill seals for furs?', following a discussion of a newspaper or television item).

★ Discuss moral dilemma stories.

• Detecting mood

★ After reading a story, ask children questions relating to the mood and tone of the story, as well as the effect it had on them (e.g. 'How did you feel when Charlotte died?', 'Why?', 'What was the saddest moment in the entire story?', 'Can you think of a part that made you happy?', 'Why?' [*Charlotte's Web*]).

• Making comparisons

★ Compare events and characters in stories, daily events, pictures, films and television programs (e.g. 'Can you think of a human character who reminds you of Wilbur?' [*Charlotte's Web*]).

• Determining character traits

★ Ask children to suggest traits possessed by a specific character (e.g. Dr McGurk in *The Super Roo of Mungalongaloo*). List traits on the board as they are suggested, then eliminate those that children cannot agree on.

✪ Ask specific questions relating to characters in stories, films and television programs (e.g. 'What do you think of Edmund?', 'Why?', 'How should Edmund change his ways?', 'Why?' [*The Lion, the Witch and the Wardrobe*]).

• Understanding the special features of language

✪ After (or while) reading a story or extract, discuss special features of the language used:
* homographs, e.g. tear;
* homophones, e.g. eight–ate;
* homonyms, e.g. fly;
* synonyms; and
* antonyms.

• Drawing conclusions

✪ While (or after) reading a story, ask questions that require children to draw a conclusion on the basis of the information in the story (e.g. 'How could the forest have grown in Max's room?', 'What possible explanations are there?' [*Where the Wild Things Are*]).

✪ Show children an editorial cartoon (e.g. Benier cartoon), and ask them to draw a conclusion based on the information contained in it. For example, remove the caption and ask: 'What is the cartoonist trying to tell us?'

• Applying information to a new situation

✪ Ask open-ended questions that require children to read 'beyond the lines' (e.g. 'What other methods might the townspeople have used to remove the rats from Hamlyn?').

✪ Ask children to use information from a story, film or television program to design, compose or prepare something original. For example, after reading *Charlie and the Chocolate Factory*, ask children to design a factory for making flying sandshoes, supersonic skateboards, packets of crisps that never empty, etc.

Written comprehension

• Recalling details from a story

✪ Have children read a story then answer simple literal questions about it (e.g. 'What did the wild thing decide to do with Max?' [*Where the Wild Things Are*]).

• Determining the main idea

✪ Have the children read a story then suggest alternative titles for it.

✪ Ask children to write appropriate captions for pictures or single frame cartoons.

• Determining character traits

⊛ Ask children to underline in pencil the topic sentence of a short extract. School magazines and photocopied extracts are ideal for this purpose.

⊛ Ask children to describe a character from a story.

⊛ Ask children to select a person (acquaintance, famous person, family member or friend) who reminds them of a specific character in a story. Ask them to explain how the characters are alike.

• Identifying simple relationships of sequence and time

⊛ Give children a sequence of events from a story, and ask them to arrange them in order.

⊛ **Paragraph shuffle** Cut up a short extract into paragraphs, then ask children to place them in correct order. A good variation of this is to write short paragraphs (or sentences) that correspond to the main details in a story and ask children to order them. Any piece of children's literature can be used in this way.

⊛ Cut up a cartoon strip, and remove the speech from the balloons (use correcting fluid). Duplicate then ask children to arrange the frames in sequence and write in each speech balloon.

• Making simple comparisons

⊛ Ask children to compare characters or events in a story (e.g. 'If you had to be one of the characters in the story, who would you like to be?', 'Why?', 'Who would be the most popular person in this story?', 'How can you tell?').

• Determining whether real or imaginary

⊛ Ask children to list things that could only be imaginary in a story. For example, following the reading of *Dr Dolittle*, ask children to list all the things that could not happen in the real world.

• Determining significant details

⊛ Provide children with a list of facts from an extract, or have them suggest details that can be written on the board. Following a short discussion, ask children to select the most significant details.

⊛ **Prepare outlines** Ask children to select an appropriate extract related to a topic, read it, write down the main idea, and then list six to ten significant details that support it.

• Making a judgement about the content of a story or extract

⊛ Ask open-ended questions that require children to make a value judgement concerning the characters or events in a story (e.g. 'Do you think Professor Branestawm was a considerate person?', 'Why or why not?', 'How do you feel about the way the Professor treated Mrs Flittersnoop?', 'How would Mrs Flittersnoop have felt about the Professor?', 'Should she have felt this way?' [*Professor Branestawm*]).

Stage 4: Independent reading

(10.0 to 12 + years approx.)

The adage that children should 'stop learning to read and start reading to learn' at a certain age is probably quite appropriate at this stage. However, to aid this learning process they will require help with higher-level comprehension skills. While many of these skills will be dealt with through discussion following the child's reading, you should provide frequent opportunities to further their understanding and interpretation of their reading through written activities. Remember, writing is a valuable aid to learning, so use it wherever appropriate to aid the thinking process, which is a part of reading.

SKILLS	ACTIVITIES

Oral comprehension

- Recalling significant details

⊛ Following a story, film, television program or other experience, ask children to suggest all the important details they can. You should conduct this as a brainstorming session, playing *all* ideas on the board or overhead projector. As children discuss each detail, look for duplication or points of secondary importance.

⊛ Following a story, ask individual children to recall everything they can about the story. As a variation, perhaps ask the child to record it on tape, so that later he/she can pick out the important ideas and perhaps prepare a short talk or summary, using the significant details. Children may also do this in pairs.

- Dramatising stories heard

⊛ Select a child, or group of children, to dramatise a story (or section of it). They may:

  * relate the story from a personal viewpoint (e.g. answering the question, 'How does it relate to my life?');
  * dramatise their favourite part;
  * present a portrayal of one character in the story;

* prepare a dialogue between two characters in the story;
* dramatise how the story line, the language or the ending of the story might be changed; or
* dramatise the whole story.

• Reasoning: Why? How? When?

✪ During (or following) a story, film, television program, science experiment or first-hand experience, ask children open-ended questions that go beyond simple observation or reporting (e.g. 'Why might one animal be fiercer and more aggressive than any other?', 'How might the wild dogs have been controlled without killing them?' [*Island of the Blue Dolphin*]; or 'How might we put the sea to better use? Think of as many ideas as you can in 5 minutes').

✪ Use the PMI approach (de Bono 1973). Suggest ideas to children, and ask them to think of all the positive (P), negative (M for minus) and interesting (I) things they can about the idea (e.g. 'There should not be any television between 4.00 p.m. and 6.00 p.m.').

✪ **Simulation games** Ask a small group of children to pretend that they are in a life raft that can support only three people. Each child has to give reasons why he/she should stay in the raft and not be thrown overboard. It may be useful to give each person a label (e.g. reporter, doctor, engineer, meteorologist).

• Anticipating outcomes

✪ Ask children to predict the end of a story before you reach it.

✪ Ask children to predict the sequel to a book or story you have read (e.g. 'What might a sequel for *Charlotte's Web* be like?'). Ask them to suggest a title for this book and then to outline, in point form, its story line.

✪ **Group storytelling** Start a fictitious story, then ask children (with no preparation) to keep adding to it. For example, perhaps start by saying: 'It all began one crisp winter morning with a visit from Dr Peter Starstruck, the Director of the National Space Laboratory ...'

✪ Have children complete cartoon strips that have had the final frame removed.

• Making a judgement concerning story content

✪ During (or following) a story, ask questions that require children to make a value judgement (e.g. 'Was the treatment of German people living in America during World War II fair?' [*The Summer of my German Soldier*]).

✪ Discussing controversial issues – allow small groups (either with or without your involvement) to discuss special issues (e.g. 'Is the mining of oil on the Great Barrier Reef desirable?', 'What are the arguments for and against this?').

• Understanding figurative language

✪ After reading a story or extract, ask questions like: 'What does the author mean by ...?', 'How could we say this another way?', 'Can you think of a similar line?' This may involve examining:
* analogies;
* popular phrases (e.g. *up a blind alley*);
* colloquialisms (e.g. *strike while the iron's hot*); and
* similes (e.g. *as fast as a rabbit*).

• Understanding the special features of language

✪ While (or after) reading a story or extract, discuss special features of language, such as:
* **homographs** (words spelt like each other, but with different meanings, e.g. tear, bow);
* words derived from other languages (e.g. *television* and *video,* from Greek *tele* = far and Latin *visio* = sight, *videre* = to see);
* words borrowed from other languages (e.g. *cafe, pizza*); and
* words that have originated in the technological age (e.g. *teflon, nylon, bitumen*).

• Making critical judgements about the author's purpose

✪ Show newspaper editorial cartoons on an overhead projector (e.g. Benier cartoons), and ask: 'Why has the cartoonist drawn this?', 'What is he/she trying to say?'

✪ From a newspaper or magazine, read a letter to the editor to children, then ask: 'Why has the author written this letter?', 'What was his/her main purpose?'

✪ Discuss specific aspects of a story you have read to children. (e.g. 'Why does the author keep saying "... she had, of course, left the door [of the wardrobe] open, for she knew that it is a very silly thing to shut oneself into a wardrobe"?' [*The Lion, the Witch and the Wardrobe*].)

• Detecting bias

✪ Examine newspaper articles on the same topic in different newspapers. Ask children to read the articles and determine whether they present the same picture. If they do not, ask: 'What are the differences?', 'Is bias shown?', 'How can we decide what the facts are?'

✪ Examine headlines of newspaper articles. Ask children to compare the impression created by the headline with the facts in the article that follows. Ask: 'Is there a discrepancy?'

✪ Examine a newspaper advertisement (on overhead projector, if multiple copies are un-available), and ask children: 'What argument is used to sell the product?', 'Is it an honest argument, based on fact?'

• Identifying contradictory material

✪ Read a newspaper editorial, extract or letter containing contradictory material. Ask children to point out the contradictions.

• Evaluating ideas for truth, logic and validity

✪ Newspaper articles and editorials are useful for these skills also. Select material that has a clear argument, and ask children questions like: 'Do you think the author is telling the truth?', 'Does his/her argument make sense?', 'Why or why not?'

✪ Following (or during) a television program (a current affairs program is ideal) or film, ask questions that require children to think about the logic of any argument used.

✪ Ask children to evaluate talks by fellow pupils, for truth and logic.

Written comprehension

• Recalling details from a story

✪ Following the reading of a story, ask children questions about it that require purely literal recall (e.g. 'What was the name of the girl whom Jennifer and Elizabeth did not like?', 'What was the last item Jennifer asked Elizabeth to place in the magic potion?' [*Jennifer, Hecate, Macbeth and Me*]).

✪ Following the reading of a story or extract, ask children to write down everything they can remember about it. As an extension, they may rework their initial notes to present a coherent picture of the content of the reading.

• Determining the main idea

✪ Ask children to write appropriate captions for pictures o single frame cartoons. At this level, editorial cartoons are excellent; remove the caption w correcting fluid, and copy.

⍟ Ask children to underline topic sentences for each paragraph in an extract. Compare the positions of topic sentences in different kinds of material (e.g. newspapers, school readers, encyclopaedias).

⍟ Start a graffiti board, and encourage children to write slogans that communicate a special message relating to important world, community and school issues. (Be brave!)

• Determining character traits

⍟ Prepare 'mug sheets' for specific characters. This can be done for characters in books, television programs, newspapers, and community and world affairs.

Name : Montgomery Jones-Smythe
Alias (Common Name) : Kid Calamity
Age : 19 years
Address : Somewhere O.S. (usually)
Description : Well known lead singer for the Punk rock group "End of the Line."
Special Features : Green shoulder-length hair; always wears high heel thongs.
Unusual or Interesting Habits : Lives almost entirely on an egg drink made with cola.

⍟ Ask children to describe specific characters in a story, by listing all their main characteristics.

• Identifying simple relationships of sequence and time

⍟ Present a series of sentences or paragraphs that outline a story they have just read. Ask children to arrange these in correct sequence.

⍟ Ask children to outline in point form the major events in a story.

⍟ Ask children to draw a time line showing how events unfolded within a specific story. (The material should be suited to this activity.)

⍟ Ask children to draw a cartoon strip that reflects the story line in a book or extract they have just read.

⍟ Following the reading of a story or extract, ask a group of children to prepare a group retelling of it.

• Making simple comparisons

⍟ Following (or during) the reading of a story, ask children questions that require them to compare characters or events (e.g. 'What is the relationship of the four children in the story?', 'Who seems to be the dominant person?',

'Which one of the children is most like you?'
[*The Lion, the Witch and the Wardrobe*]).

❊ Ask children to compare story content with other stories, or with events in their own lives.

• Determining significant details

❊ After children have read a story, viewed a television program or film, or listened to a prepared talk by a fellow pupil, ask them to list everything they can remember about it. Then ask them to rework their notes, to eliminate less important points and to reorder more important details according to significance.

❊ Ask children to prepare skeleton outlines of a book, film, television program or oral presentation. These outlines may take the following forms:

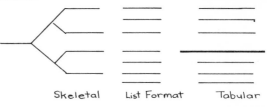

Skeletal   List Format   Tabular

• Making a judgement about the content of a story or extract

❊ Ask open-ended questions that require children to make a value judgement concerning the characters or events in a story (e.g. 'Do you think the practice of sending children off to the country away from their parents during the War was justified?' [*The Lion, the Witch and the Wardrobe*]).

• Anticipating outcomes

❊ Stop children before they reach the end of a story, and ask them to write down how they feel that the story will end. This may be in point form or essay form.

• Drawing conclusions

❊ Following the reading of a story, ask children to draw specific conclusions based on its content (e.g. 'Why do you think Jennifer kept deceiving Elizabeth for so long that she was a witch?' [*Jennifer, Hecate, Macbeth and Me*]).

• Determining whether fact or opinion

❊ Have children read an advertisement and list the qualities of a product. Then ask them to divide these statements between fact and opinion.

❊ Ask children to read an extract (e.g. from a story or newspaper) and underline the points that are purely opinion.

- Determining whether relevant or irrelevant

✪ Ask children to read an extract and then quickly write down everything that supports its main topic. Ask them then to go through and select only the most relevant points to place in a summary.

✪ Provide an extract with a clear argument (e.g. letter to the editor), and ask children to divide the statements into those that are highly relevant to the argument and those that are of limited relevance.

- Applying information to a new situation

✪ Ask children open-ended questions that require them to apply the content of a piece of reading to a new situation. For example, following the reading of *Professor Branestawm*, ask children to draw a special machine that the professor might have invented, label it and explain how it works. Perhaps ask them to explain how it might be constructed.

✪ Ask children to take the content of a story and change it in some way (e.g. 'Write a short [serious] newspaper article based on the content of *The Lion, the Witch and the Wardrobe*').

- Preparing a logical sequel or preview to a story

✪ Ask children to prepare a book review that will make other readers want to read the book. Publish these in a class book, so that children can seek further information about books to read (perhaps also use a card system).

✪ Following the reading of a story, ask children to outline in point form the story line that a sequel for this book might take.

- Suggesting alternative solutions to problems raised in reading material

✪ Ask children specific questions related to problems encountered in a story (e.g. 'What logical explanation might there be for a group of children's finding a magic land by entering a wardrobe?', 'Is it possible for someone to fly using his own power?', 'How might this be done?', 'What are the different solutions?'.

Three special techniques that develop comprehension ability

As you have probably realised from the above activities and discussion, most of the strategies used in the classroom help to develop many skills at the same time. The following are techniques that encourage children to become actively involved in reading as a thinking process. Probably few methods provide greater opportunity for the child to develop comprehension skills.

Cloze techniques

Cloze involves deleting specific words (or parts of words) from a sentence, extract or story. Children are then required to fill the gap with a word that 'makes sense'. You should accept any response that is both syntactically and semantically correct. The advantage of the cloze procedure is that it can require the child to use all his reading strategies to complete the text.

Cloze can be used:
* orally;
* silently;
* individually; and
* in groups (a group works co-operatively through an extract, adding appropriate words).

You can delete:
* words at random;
* words at regular intervals (every sixth, eighth, tenth or fifteenth word —not too many initially);
* parts of words (leave in initial or final letter clues, e.g. *b*_____, _____-*ing*); or
* specific words.

Cloze can be a powerful tool if a child shows a specific misuse of contextual information (e.g. miscues when reading with words that consistently are syntactically correct but destroy the meaning; or miscues by using words that are correct for the preceding text, but not the text that follows). For specific problems like this, you can design special cloze activities. For example:
* Delete only content words (nouns, verbs, adjectives, adverbs), thus encouraging the child to search for meaning (e.g. Billy caught the _____ to the beach. His friend Paul always got on at Ashfield _____).
* Delete only structural words (conjunctions, pronouns, articles, prepositions), thus encouraging the reader to use his/her knowledge of language to select words that are syntactically correct. (e.g. Before Harold left, _____ remembered to water the garden and feed _____ cat).
* Leave in certain sounds when the word is deleted (beginning sounds, end sounds, consonants only). This encourages the reader to use all reading strategies at once.

A few special points and ideas
* Start initially with oral cloze.
* When working with young children (or when using material for the first time), make sure that the material is interesting and the language natural.
* Use a variety of material for cloze exercises:
  * stories;
  * nonfiction;
  * rhymes and jingles;

* language experience stories;
* rhyming poetry;
* songs; and
* captions and labels.
● Cloze can be used even with very young children. Perhaps start by using:
  * captions around the room (e.g. 'Our fish _____ here');
  * rhymes and jingles (e.g. 'Meadow Lea, you ought to be _____',
  'Jack and Jill _____ up the hill');
  * children's own dictated stories; and
  * songs and poems children know (create a new version).
● Do not select material that is difficult or lacking in interest.

Rebus technique

Rebus is a variation of the cloze approach and is excellent for beginning or poor readers. Instead of leaving a blank when a word is deleted, replace it with a picture. The main problem with the rebus technique is that the exercises take a lot of time to prepare. However, some commercial materials are now available; and in any case, it is not difficult to use rebus in a limited way. For example:
● Quickly write on the board a single sentence with a single picture in it (e.g. 'Kathy likes to ___ the fence').
● Change the drawing, accepting any response that makes sense.
● Use rebus in reverse; that is, supply short sentences with a gap, and ask children to draw an appropriate picture in the space.
● Use rebus in functional reading activities (e.g. a recipe for chocolate crackles, the procedure for making jelly cups, the instructions for making a party hat). Make a large version of the instructions on chart paper (or the board) for children to follow while doing the activity.

Integrated story treatment

I did not know quite what to call this approach, as for years I have used it without a label. Similar approaches, with a variety of names (e.g. Directed Reading Thinking Activities), have been suggested by other people. Whatever the technique is called, it has proven to be very useful with children of all ages.

Once you have selected an appropriate piece of reading that children have not seen before, you are ready to start. All children need the same material, so group work is essential. Basal readers are suitable for this purpose.

You may use one session or several sessions. Each session will be characterised by continual swapping from reading to talking (and vice versa). There are three clear stages in the strategy:

Stage 1   The first stage, doing things *before* reading, is designed to cue children into the content of the material they will read. The provision of advance organisers (e.g. questions, a summary paragraph introducing the content, a specific purpose for reading, a picture) and discussion help to give children an appropriate mental set for reading.

Stage 2   The second stage, doing things *while* reading (e.g. reading, talking, reading, writing, reading . . .) is designed to encourage children actively to think about the content of the story as they read.

Stage 3   The third stage, doing things *after* reading, is designed to encourage children to reflect upon their reading, do some wider reading and further their development in language.

The easiest way to give a clear indication of this approach is to show a lesson plan (in reality it was several lessons) I have used.

A lesson using integrated story treatment

This example relates to a story that forms part of the Endeavour Reading Scheme (level 15), namely, 'The too-many professors' by Norman Hunter (from *Professor Branestawm*).

Stage 1: Preparation for reading

Discussion   Read the introduction to the class (provided in the reader), then ask questions such as the following:

• What does the name *Professor Branestawm* suggest to you? Does the word *Brane-stawm* give you any clue as to the type of person the Professor was?

• Look at the picture on page 17 of the reader. Does that give you an indication of the type of person Professor Branestawm was? What about the character Mrs Flittersnoop?

• Would it be exciting to be an inventor? Why? or Why not?

• What would you invent if given the opportunity? Think about the problems your invention might cause.

Language preparation

• Discuss the names *Professor Branestawm, Mrs Flittersnoop, Colonel Dedshott* and *Catapult Cavaliers*. Examine the words they are derived from, as well as the significance of these words. Invent some other names.

• Examine and discuss the words *inventory, syringe, bacteria, cinders* and *scoundrel*. See whether children can derive meaning by using the context (e.g. burned themselves into *cinders*).

• Discuss the invented sound words (e.g. *pw-o-ough, Oo-er, Phiz-z-z-z, pr-r-r-r-ing-g, zzzzzzzzp*).

• Discuss the invented word *professorish*. Attempt to derive meaning from context. Discuss the reasons for its use.

• Examine the multiple meanings of *blotting*. Examine each in context.

Stage 2: Directed Reading

Reading for a purpose   Tell children: 'I want you to read up to page 20 to find out exactly the type of people Professor Branestawm and Mrs Flittersnoop were. When we finish, we'll list all their characteristics.'

Audience reading   Ask some children to read the story together (orally) in order to select a section to be prepared for audience reading to the group.

Stage 3: Follow-up to reading

Oral comprehension   In effect, a great deal of questioning is done during stage 2. However, it also can follow the reading. Always have a good balance of questions (i.e. literal, interpretive, critical and creative). The following are some sample questions:

• What was the Professor's latest invention? (literal)
• Why did Mrs Flittersnoop worry about the apples and chocolates she ate? (interpretive)
• If you were asked to describe Professor Branestawm (not just his appearance) to a friend who knew nothing about him, how would you do it (in no more than two or three sentences)? (interpretive)
• How do you think Mrs Flittersnoop felt about the Professor? Did she like him? (interpretive)
• Should the Professor have considered Mrs Flittersnoop's feelings more when conducting all his wild experiments? (critical)
• Imagine that someone did invent a solution like the Professor's and could make people in photographs come to life. Should someone be allowed to use such an invention? (critical)
• What might the Professor's next invention be? Draw it. Add labels to explain all its working parts. (creative)

Reading activities   These can be either group or individual activities. Offer a number of alternatives, such as the following:

• Prepare a monologue, pretending that you are one of the characters in the story.
• Write another ending for the story.
• Prepare an interview (on tape). You are a radio reporter interviewing one of the three characters after the people changed back into photographs.
• Prepare an advertisement that attempts to sell one of the Professor's inventions.
• Draw one of the characters from the story, or draw the scene in the house as the people started emerging from the photograph album.
• Prepare a newspaper account of the incidents following the spilling of the secret formula.

Recreational reading   Encourage children to read the complete book 'The too-many professors' is taken from (*Professor Branestawm*), as well as others in the series:

   • *The Incredible Adventures of Professor Branestawm*
   • *The Peculiar Triumph of Professor Branestawm*
   • *Professor Branestawm's Compendium*
   • *Professor Branestawm's Dictionary*
   • *Professor Branestawm's Great Revolution*
   • *Professor Branestawm's Treasure Hunt.*

CHAPTER FIVE
Reading for a variety of purposes

This chapter is included to heighten your awareness of the variable nature of the reading process created by different audiences and purposes for reading.

Reading clearly places different demands upon the reader when it occurs in different contexts. Consider the variation between each of these reading situations:

- reading a story for pleasure;
- reading a story orally as part of a group;
- reading a prepared piece of literature to the entire class;
- reading own written work to a school assembly;
- reading a story out loud to an adult (e.g. mother);
- reading the instructions on a model aeroplane packet;
- reading a bus timetable to find specific information;
- reading and searching through a directory for specific information (e.g. Yellow Pages in telephone directory); and
- reading an encyclopaedia to find specific information.

This is hardly an exhaustive list, but it does indicate the diversity that exists. The child reading a book for pleasure has different constraints from the child reading a rehearsed piece of literature to a school assembly.

In the latter case, the reader will be concerned far more with accurately communicating the text exactly as it is written on the page. He/she will also strive to aid the communication of the author's message by adding expression and perhaps even non-verbal gestures.

However, the child reading for pleasure is able to sample less print, because only he/she now has to understand the message; it does not have to be communicated to another audience. In this situation, the reader will probably substitute or omit parts of the text while reading; this would not be appropriate if it were being presented to a group.

Even reading situations that appear essentially the same can place different demands upon the reader. For example, reading instructions relating to the construction of a model is quite different from reading instructions on a vending machine. While both involve a series of steps that must be understood and executed, they are different in a number of ways.

In reading the instructions on a model, the process is essentially one of reading an instruction, carrying it out, reading some further instructions, assimilating these with the previous step (and the knowledge gained by executing it), then performing another step. This stopping and starting continues as the reader progressively interprets each instruction in the light of what has preceded it.

However, the operation of a vending machine usually involves synthesising all instructions 'in the reader's head' before attempting the task. In fact, often it involves simply looking at one or two instructions before executing the task; the reader combines this information with prior knowledge of vending machines, to operate it successfully.

It should not be assumed that all readers would read in these situations in exactly the same way. Clearly, even in the above examples there is room for great variation. Even the single factor of prior knowledge of the type of reading task (e.g. how many models the child has done before) can have an important influence on the types of demands placed on the reader. It cannot even be assumed that a single reader would perform the same task in the same way each time. Think about the different demands each of the following activities would put upon the reader:

• using a public phone for the first time to ring a friend, *compared with* using it for the first time as the result of an emergency; and

• reading out loud as part of an oral reading group, *compared with* reading out loud to a teacher as part of reading assessment.

Clearly, the reading process is complex, and many factors affect the reader's ability to extract meaning from print. All these (i.e. contextual factors, reading purpose, prior knowledge) interact to place different demands on the reader for different types of reading. We cannot always assume, then, that frequent opportunities to read will be sufficient to develop each child's ability to read for a variety of purposes and for different audiences.

Your main responsibility, in the light of the above discussion, is to provide frequent opportunities for children to experience reading in a variety of forms and contexts. Numerous opportunities arise in every classroom to provide opportunities for wider reading experiences of this type; ideally, they will be introduced as an outcome of other activities. The following are examples of various reading activities you may provide:

• locating information from directories (e.g. telephone, accommodation), catalogues, dictionaries, encyclopaedias, maps, manuals, newspapers, magazines and timetables;

• following sets of instructions relating to toys, models, games, machines, and cooking recipes;

• reading aloud reports, stories, poems, self-written work and jokes (provide further variation by varying the audience, e.g. partner, small group, school assembly, parents, teacher, parent group);

- reading and completing simple forms;
- using special study techniques (e.g. skimming, previewing, note making);
- reading and using library catalogues, tables of contents and indexes; and
- reading silently for pleasure.

While your main role is simply to provide opportunities for reading of this type, there are obviously useful skills that are necessary for most of these specific forms of reading. You will often need to help children in each of these skill areas. The following outline may prove useful to help you to focus attention on some of these skills, as children read. For convenience and clarity, they are grouped into three main categories:

- locating information;
- oral and audience reading; and
- recreational reading.

Locating information

SKILLS

ACTIVITIES

Sequencing skills

- Locating and sequencing information, using alphabetical order

✪ Provide simple picture dictionaries for children to locate words in.

✪ Provide a blank book for children to use as a personal dictionary (mark pages in alphabetical order for them).

✪ Ask children to locate specific words in a simple dictionary.

✪ Ask children to locate specific pieces of information in an encyclopaedia.

✪ Provide opportunities for children to find a specific name in a telephone directory.

✪ Ask children to find a specific piece of information, using an index in a reference book.

✪ Have children find a specific item (using the alphabetical index) in the Yellow Pages (e.g. *public schools*).

✪ Ask children to find a specific book, using a library card catalogue.

- Locating information using temporal order

✪ Introduce a weekly class timetable, and write significant events on it. Ask children to tell you events that will take place soon (e.g. next important event for the class, next lunch monitor).

✪ Display a daily class timetable on which you place special activities. Ask children to tell you, for example, what time something is planned for, what special activity is next, or what has to be done *after* lunch.

⭐ Ask children to find specific dates on a yearly calendar. Ask them questions like: 'When will our school term end?', 'Who is having a birthday next week?', 'How many birthdays are there in March?', 'On what date is the October long-weekend holiday?'

⭐ Using a television guide, ask children to find specific pieces of information (e.g. 'What time of the day is 'Sale of the Century' on at?', 'What is the last program on Channel 7 on Thursday night?', 'At what time does it start?', 'What five programs (on two separate channels) could you watch after school?', 'What is the first program after the news each night on Channel 9?').

⭐ Using bus or train timetables (perhaps make up your own at first), ask children to answer specific questions about travelling (e.g. 'How many different buses could you catch to school each morning, to arrive between 8.30 a.m. and 9.15 a.m.?', 'At what time would you have to catch a bus, if you wanted to travel to Grundig on a Saturday morning?', 'How many trains travel from Grundig to Catchem each day?').

• Understanding and following instructions

⭐ Children's ability to follow instructions is obviously influenced by the difficulty of the task to be performed, the clarity and completeness of the instructions, and also their experience of the task concerned. Provide opportunities for children to experience instructions of slowly increasing complexity. Activities may include the following:

Treasure hunt   Help children to plan a treasure hunt, following a sequence of simple instructions (e.g. 'Walk ten steps towards the carpark from the classroom door; turn and walk forty steps until you see a small tree ...'). Provide verbal directions at first.

Cooking   Provide a cooking activity that requires children to follow a series of simple written steps (e.g. 'Fill a jug with warm water; pour contents of jelly crystals into jug ...'). The use of rebus techniques is useful for this purpose.

Games   Ask a small group to read the instruc-

tions for a simple game (e.g. Ludo) and then explain them (in simple terms) to the class.

Washing Ask children to read, in pairs, the instructions on a number of laundry products (e.g. spray-on starch) and then rewrite the instructions in their own words for other children to follow.

Do-it-yourself Present the instructions for a specific product from a hardware store (e.g. glue, paint, plaster filler) on separate cards. Ask children to rearrange, in pairs, the instructions in correct sequence.

Model construction Provide a set of instructions for a model or construction toy to a group of children and ask them to construct it. Obviously, there are limitless possibilities in this area. Always try to make it fun; and if possible, let the children actually perform the tasks.

✪ Hold theme days. Perhaps talk about:
  * food (ask pupils to bring food in packets and tins);
  * laundry products (e.g. washing detergent, floor cleansers);
  * medical products (e.g. throat lozenges, aspirins, crepe bandages);
  * games (e.g. Monopoly, Hungry Hippos, electronic games, card games);
  * machines (e.g. battery toys, construction toys, vegetable slicer);
  * kits (e.g. model aeroplanes);
  * manuals;
  * newspapers; and
  * magazines.

Activities for theme days may include:
  * collecting ideas related to a specific topic to prepare a talk to be given to the class;
  * using a single reference book to find out about a specific topic, and making a list of ten important points;
  * reading the relevant sections in several books on one topic in order to prepare a short outline;
  * locating specific telephone numbers in a telephone book;
  * locating the name of a specific firm in the Yellow Pages of a telephone book;

* locating the name of the motel offering cheapest accommodation in the Sydney area, using a single directory;
* locating a specific item in the classified section of a newspaper (e.g. the cheapest refrigerator, the cheapest Holden car that is no more than five years old);
* locating specific information in certain sections of the newspaper (e.g. the results of all the reserve-grade rugby league games, the winner of the VFL match of the day); and
* selecting the best buy in BMX bikes from several toy catalogues (children must give sound reasons for their choice, not just price).

The above ideas are simply examples. Variety is important.

✸ Hold a mini-excursion, visiting:
* lolly-vending machines;
* automatic stamp machines; and
* telephones (ring the secretary at school).

Location skills

• Understanding and using parts of a book

✸ Children should understand all parts of a book:

Table of contents   Show children how to use the table of contents to locate a specific story, to anticipate the contents of the book, and to select specific information relating to a topic.

Index   Show children how to find a specific topic in the book, using the index. Point out the use of topic headings and author names.

Glossary   Show children how to use the glossary to determine the meaning of specific terms as they are used in context.

• Locating information from a variety of written materials

✸ One of the most important skills that independent readers must acquire is the ability to locate information. You should give children the opportunity to apply their location skills using a variety of material, which should include:
* reference books;
* catalogues; and
* directories.

Try using a group project approach:

Plan a holiday   Ask children (in groups of two to four) to plan a holiday using road maps, timetables, travel brochures and holiday accommodation directories. Perhaps impose specific limits (e.g. you would like to fly; it must be within Australia; you have fourteen days; you are taking two adults with you; you have $3000 to spend).

Furnish a house Provide children with department store catalogues and several weekend newspapers, and ask them to select furniture for a house. The house has three bedrooms and a lounge, dining room, family room, kitchen, bathroom and laundry. They have $5000 to spend. They must stretch their money to cover as many essential items as possible.

Spend, spend, spend Ask children to imagine that they have just won $2000 in a competition. They must decide what to spend it on, using several weekend newspapers and a variety of catalogues.

- Locating specific books in a library

✪ Ask children to locate a book, using the title as a guide.

✪ Give children a book title and author's name, and ask them to find the book on the fiction shelves.

✪ Using the library catalogue, give children the name of one book, and ask them to find three others covering a similar topic. They must record the titles, authors' names and call numbers before using these books to obtain specific information concerning the topic.

- Using and interpreting pictorial sources of information

✪ You should help children fully to understand and use:
  * illustrations;
  * graphs;
  * diagrams;
  * charts;
  * timelines; and
  * maps (including simple keys and scales).

The many activities you may use to develop these skills include:
  * using a simple map for a treasure hunt;
  * examining a simple column graph and asking children questions like: 'Who scored the most points in athletics?', 'Which house had

the highest combined swimming and athletics score?';
* asking children to locate specific features on a map, using a grid reference;
* estimating the distance between towns on a map, using the key;
* placing the events in a story on a simple time line; and
* using a map to locate places mentioned in a story.

Study skills

• Skimming to get a general idea of the content

⊛ This useful skill enables the reader quickly to survey a large volume of reading material. It can be applied at a number of different levels and for a variety of purposes. Activities may include:
* skimming tables of contents to obtain a general idea of content;
* skimming a chapter to survey headings, to gain an overview of its content; and
* skimming a book to check whether it is relevant to a specific topic.

• Scanning a piece of reading material to find a specific piece of information

⊛ This skill, like skimming, can be used at a variety of levels. Activities may include:
* scanning an extract to find an answer to a specific question;
* scanning a chapter to find a heading or key word relating to a specific topic;
* scanning a story to find a specific piece of information (e.g. the description of _____ pony); and
* scanning an index to find a specific topic quickly.

• Using the SQ3R technique

⊛ This technique is closely related to the above skills, because it uses both of them. The procedure for using it, devised by Robinson (1961), involves a number of clear steps:
Step 1: Survey   The reader quickly examines the entire extract or book. If a book, he/she examines the title, subheadings, pictures etc. A good idea initially is to set a time limit (e.g. 2 minutes) to survey a book. This step provides a quick idea of content and is very useful if you are teaching children to select appropriate reference books.

Step 2: Question The reader is asked to formulate several questions he/she thinks that the extract or book is likely to answer, or questions he/she would like answered. The reader may also write these down. This step acts as a valuable advance organiser and cues the reader into the reading task.

Step 3: Read The reader reads the material, perhaps making brief notes as he/she goes. Sometimes it is useful if the reader places key words next to the original questions.

Step 4: Recite This step requires the reader to attempt to recite answers from memory for each original question (without notes at first). If still unsure, the reader rereads the piece.

Step 5: Review At a later stage (perhaps when he/she has to write notes for a project), the reader goes back over his/her notes, or quickly skims the material to prepare for note making or a talk to a group.

This approach is difficult for most primary-school children if used exactly as outlined above. A much better approach is to modify this strategy to suit the needs of your children (e.g. Survey, Question, Read). Ideally, give a number of group oral lessons on this strategy before encouraging children to use it themselves.

• Making notes and summarising

⊛ Ask children to select three or four topics to study during an excursion. Get them to compose an appropriate question for each topic before proceeding to collect information relating to each. Ask them to restrict their notes to ten points on each question.

⊛ Have children use a prepared sheet with spaces to record the main idea (or topic) of material they are reading. Provide space for ten to fifteen significant points about the topic, and room for a fifty-word summary. You should precede work on this written skill by a number of group oral lessons.

⊛ Ask children to prepare outlines, following the reading of an extract. As mentioned in Chapter 4 (p. 57), perhaps use skeletal, tabular or list approaches.

⊛ Following the reading of several extracts or

books, show children how to combine notes they have made:

    * A useful technique is to get children to record separate points on small pieces of cardboard or paper. Have a group sit down after the notes have been made and try to combine them. Let them shuffle them, group them, throw some away. The child who wrote the notes has the right to veto any decision, but must give a clear justification for doing so. Eventually, children will perform this task themselves.

    * Show them other methods as well (e.g. cut and paste, 'scribble and scratch', using a numbering system to show the sequence of ideas for rewriting).

★ Try getting children to wait until they have finished an extract before quickly writing down every important point they can think of. Demonstrate how they can then reread in order to edit the notes made.

★ Have children write down only key words while reading. When they have finished reading, ask them to 'fill out' each point from memory, using a tree diagram approach:

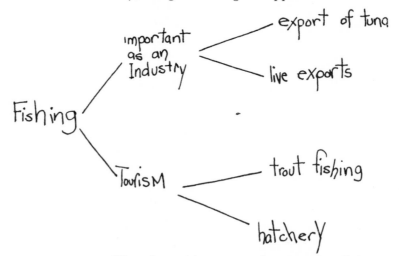

The above ideas are only examples. Primary children have to be given frequent opportunities to practise their note-making skills. An important point to remember is that written activities should be preceded by many oral lessons.

Oral and audience reading

Oral reading is perhaps the most abused form of reading in classrooms. Often it is the primary strategy for reading development. Traditionally, oral reading has been used widely as a group strategy at all grade levels.

Obviously, the use of oral reading does have some advantages:
• It is a simple way to ensure that children read daily.
• It is an effective way to obtain feedback relating to the way children read.
• It is an efficient way to free teachers to provide more intensive work for other children.

However, it should be recognised that proficient readers rarely have to read orally; most reading is conducted silently. Furthermore, as the discussion in Chapter 1 has shown, the oral-reading and silent-reading processes are quite different.

Oral reading requires the reader to process print and then decode it into sound. However, **silent reading** requires the reader purely to process print to obtain meaning. The absence of the 'decoding to sound' step enables the reader to be more actively involved in a search for meaning: leaving words out, adding extra words and substituting words. The reader is thus freed to use far more contextual analysis, and reading becomes more of a thinking process.

Consequently, children should be given far greater opportunities to read silently. This does not mean that oral reading should be ignored. For the beginning reader, oral reading is very important. In fact, most children in their first year of reading will have difficulty reading silently. As a result, oral reading will be the principal reading mode for most beginning readers.

If you use oral reading, you should observe a few rules:
• Do not have children involved continually in round-the-group reading without your involvement.
• Do not use it in groups where children have vastly different reading abilities. Let us avoid the 'Miss, I've lost the place' reaction.
• Always use reading material at the correct instructional level.
• Always select material that lends itself to oral reading.
• Try to make it fun; give children lots of positive reinforcement.
• Read along with them at times.
• Do not correct every miscue children make. In fact, do not correct any miscues that are semantically and syntactically correct.
• Any words that need to be corrected (or that need to be taught) are best dealt with at the end of the reading.
• If the child cannot identify a word within 5 seconds, supply it. You may suggest looking at the words around it, rereading the sentence or using an initial letter cue, but these strategies should not be overused.

You should remember that oral reading has a place with children of all ages. While oral reading will be used less in later life than silent reading, it will occasionally be used when reading to children (and after all, we keep trying to convince parents of the importance of this), when reading the minutes or a report at a meeting (e.g. P and C, sporting club), and when reading own work to a group (e.g. reading a section of an essay to a group in high school English, reading a prepared talk).

However, it should be pointed out that each of the above has a different purpose from that of oral reading in reading lessons. All these examples involve reading a prepared piece for a special purpose to a special audience; this is **audience reading**.

Audience reading is obviously a worthwhile form of reading to include as part of your program. Children still need to be given the opportunity to develop the necessary skills that will enable them to read a prepared piece to a specific audience. Some of these important skills are:

• reading orally in units of meaning;
• understanding the function of simple punctuation;
• reading fluently;
• reading clearly and distinctly;
• using suitable and variable pitch when reading;
• reading at an appropriate rate for the purpose of the activity;
• determining and projecting the mood or tone of a piece;
• reading so that listeners enjoy the story; and
• using proper voice intonation to project meaning.

All these skills should be developed using reading activities that have a real purpose. The development of each skill is very much interrelated. The following are some ideas and activities for developing audience-reading skills:

Reading to a variety of audiences   Encourage children to read to:
• their parents;
• a partner;
• a group of children;
• the class;
• a younger class;
• you;
• another teacher;
• a school assembly; and
• an audience, via a tape recorder.

Reading for many different purposes   Encourage children to read:
• their own work (e.g. stories, poems, projects) to the class;
• their favourite poem;
• a story composed by a group;
• a special announcement at a school assembly;
• their favourite riddles;
• plays to the rest of the class;
• a simulated news broadcast, sports commentary or advertisement; and
• dramatic verse.

Using markers   To encourage children to read fluently and in units of meaning, perhaps:
• replace their finger pointing (which leads to word-by-word reading) with a

ruler placed above the line of print as the child proceeds, or with a finger moving vertically down the margin; or

• place pencil slashes at appropriate pause points within the reading, to encourage children to process chunks of print rather than single words.

Phrase reading   Occasionally, you can encourage very young readers to read in units of meaning by providing them with a series of meaningful phrases or sentences they have composed. For several weeks, replace their normal reading with the reading of the phrases (e.g. *Ian had mumps; Turtles can't run; I like lots of honey; I did as Mum said; See the aeroplane up in the air*). Children will quickly compose units of this type; simply ask them to 'make up a little story with _____ in it'.

Choice of material   It is probably worth re-emphasising that it is necessary carefully to select reading materials:

• Select material that has fairly natural language. The content should be interesting and related to children's experience. This especially applies to the young or poor reader.

• Young children and poor readers should also be provided with reading material printed in units of meaning. Initially, avoid material that places parts of a meaningful chunk of print on separate lines.

Read-along strategies

Neurological impress method (NIM)   This is a technique developed by Heckelman (1969) to aid children with a variety of reading problems. It appears to be useful for promoting fluency and expression in oral reading. Use the technique the following way:

• Select a book matched closely to the child's interest, experience and reading level (pick something a little easier to start).

• Sit next to the child so that you are leaning slightly towards his/her ear.

• Read the material aloud with the child.

• Read a little more quickly, while running a finger smoothly under the print (just ahead of the word you are saying). Later, the child can do this.

• Provide daily sessions of 15 minutes. Discontinue the approach after fifteen to twenty lessons if no improvement is shown. Heckelman recommends using this approach for a maximum of thirty-two to forty-eight sessions.

A few general points:

• Provide well-graded material for the program. (Do not move too quickly.)

• Do not question after the sessions to test comprehension, but general discussion may be useful.

• Do not worry if children lose their places. Keep going; they will catch up.

• Use only well-trained instructors. Usually, you will need to use parents or older children, but use them only if they have been given clear instructions and have practised beforehand.

Taped readers   This approach is an offshoot of the above method, but it is much more useful because it does not require your involvement at all times. Furthermore, more than one child can read along if a listening post is used. It is quite easy to use this method as part of a basal program. You may like to tape stories yourself, so that each child has at least one session a week. If recording your own stories, remember the following points:

• Choose your material carefully (i.e. interesting, correct difficulty level, suitable for oral reading).

• Pace the reading carefully. Do not read too quickly, but remember that it is just as bad to read too slowly.

• Read it in clear units of meaning and with as much expression as possible.

• Use a sound to signal the end of each page (e.g. strike a glass with a spoon).

• Try to get someone else to read a story; a change of voice is useful. Parents are often ideal.

I have found the technique more useful if used intensively for a short period (four to six weeks) with children who can read but need to improve their fluency and expression. It is sometimes useful to plan other activities related to the story (e.g. word study, language activities, oral comprehension). If used intensively, it is probably a good idea to use the same story for the whole week. Children will not become bored if they feel that it is special and that they are making progress.

Special tape-recorder activities   Tape recorders may be used in other ways also:

• Provide opportunities for individual children to practise a piece by reading it onto a tape recorder.

• Ask some children to prepare a taped version of a play. Suggest playing to the class as a radio play. The group is responsible for providing backing music, introduction and any other additional material.

• Have a small group record a radio news session.

Recreational reading

There can be little doubt that the most important element in any reading program is the provision for children to read constantly. In fact, some reading educators claim that reading instruction need not involve anything else.

While many children will need assistance with the development of the skills discussed in the above sections, one of the most important things that you can do to foster children's reading development is to 'switch them on to books'. In my own classrooms, I have very rarely found a child who could not be encouraged to enjoy recreational reading.

Many factors can dampen children's enthusiasm for books, but the main ones appear to be:
• a lack of awareness that reading can be a source of pleasure (these children typically have not been read to and have not possessed their own books);
• a lack of appropriate material (interest and reading level);
• an inability to select appropriate books;
• insufficient opportunities to read without being interrupted; and
• a negative attitude towards reading caused by failure and/or inappropriate teaching methods.

Irrespective of the cause of a child's lack of interest in reading, there are many strategies you can adopt to overcome this problem. Obviously, before even considering these strategies, it is important to ensure that all children have the opportunity to *read independently for at least 15 minutes each day*.

Creating a stimulating environment   There are three main elements in the classroom reading environment:

• *Teacher–pupil relationship*   Probably one of the most important factors is the need to create a warm and supportive classroom environment in which all members show interest in each other's work. It is imperative that all children feel that you are personally interested in them. You need to convince them that you are interested in their reading development, and that you would like to know about the special books they have been reading.

• *The classroom*
  * Ensure that the classroom is bright and attractive. Decorate it with children's work, and make it an environment they are happy to be in.
  * Have a special reading board (e.g. 'Beaut books I've read'). Encourage children to record the names of books they have enjoyed.
  * Create a special activities corner where children can make and do things related to their reading. (This is discussed in detail later in this chapter.)
  * Try to find special nooks outside the room for reading (e.g. verandas, hat rooms, a favourite tree).

• *Books*   You cannot read without books. Try building up a class library by:
  * arranging bulk loans from the school and public libraries;
  * scavenging books by requesting any spare books that children have at home (loan only);

* collecting newspapers and magazines for reading (only as an alternative; avoid continued use); and

* if money is available, buying some cheap paperbacks. (Ashton Scholastic Core Libraries are useful.)

Once you have the books, you should:

* label them for ease of selection, using a colour-coded system; and

* arrange a new display each week.

Try arranging a thematic display (e.g. science fiction, animal stories).

Reading to children   Read quality literature to children every day. This is often the easiest way to make a breakthrough with the uninterested reader. The many other benefits of reading to them daily have already been discussed. Make all books you read available for pupil loan.

Helping children to select books   Based on your knowledge of children's interests (use an interest inventory early in the year) and reading ability, help them to select books. Walk with them to the bookshelves and pick out several titles that may be suitable. Ideally, say a little about each book. This requires you to have a great deal of knowledge of children's books. Read children's books yourself, so that you can develop this knowledge. Always insist that children read at least the first chapter before returning a book to the shelves.

Individual conferences   The individual conference is not only a valuable way to learn about your children; it is also an excellent way to stimulate interest in reading. Finding time to do this is sometimes a problem. Overcome it by using a variable time slot while most children are working independently (not necessarily reading). Ask children whether they would like to discuss their books. Place names in order on the board, then see children individually. Give all children an opportunity to have at least one conference a week. While conferences are not compulsory, most children will request their session each time (most will be over in no more than 5 minutes). This is a scheme I have always used.

During each session, perhaps do the following:

• List any books read on a special card. (Some have criticised this practice, but I have found it to be an excellent source of information. Children also enjoy looking at their lists.)

• Ask general questions about the books: 'Did you like them?', 'Tell me about a special incident in one of them', 'Tell me about one of the characters in each book', 'Is it like any other book you have read?' These questions should stimulate discussion and provide a check to see whether the child has read the books, *but* you should not make it seem like a checking procedure. If possible, just let the child talk.

• Ask the child to read a favourite part of one book.

• Suggest other suitable books.

Special awards   I have often made awards to avid readers. Give certificates and books for a variety of reasons, so that all children receive an award at some stage. Always emphasise personal growth, interest and variety of reading. Under no circumstances should you encourage group competition.

Library visits
• Visit the school library with children. Read with them, and help them with the selection of suitable books.
• Plan an excursion to the public library (if you have one close), and help children to join. Arrange follow-up visits if possible.

Book clubs Encourage children to join a book club. This is extremely valuable, because it gives children an opportunity inexpensively to obtain copies of books they can call their own (for some, perhaps for the first time). The Ashton Scholastic bookclubs are quite suitable.

Uninterrupted sustained silent reading (USSR) This simple technique provides children with an opportunity to read daily. It involves a number of simple steps:
• *Step 1* Choose a set time each day (short sessions at first, but gradually increasing to 15 minutes for primary children). This can be done at a class or school level.
• *Step 2* Allow children to select books in a separate time slot of 5–10 minutes (it does not have to be prior to the reading session). You may help them during this period. Perhaps teach them a simple technique for checking difficulty, such as the five-finger test: 'Open the book at the middle, and read a page. Count words you cannot read, using your fingers. If you use up all your fingers on one page, perhaps you should put the book back.'
• *Step 3* Insist that everyone reads (including yourself and all members of staff if it is done at a school level).
Observe a few simple rules:
• no talking;
• no putting a book back unless it is finished;
• no interruptions (place a sign on the door).

Special 'book chats'   Occasionally, group children with similar interests and encourage them to discuss books they have read. Perhaps group them because they have read the same book, because they are interested in the same topics, or because they have read the same author's work. Initially, you may sit in on the group to give some guidance; later, children should operate well without you. If they still find it difficult, give them a few standard procedures to follow.

Integrated activities sessions   I have used this approach often and found it extremely useful. This is how it works:

- *Step 1*   Select a one-hour session for the activities.
- *Step 2*   Set up a special activities corner, and ask children to bring in odds and ends. Explain that you are going to give them the opportunity to make or do something related to books they have read. Children may collect such items as bottle tops, wire, cardboard, plastic containers, tins, wire mesh, iceblock sticks, material, foam and wood. Add school supplies such as paint, paper, pencils, glue and brushes to the corner.
- *Step 3*   Hold your first session. Do not insist that children do anything. Allow them to read if they wish. Perhaps make some suggestions as to the type of things they might do.

The following ideas provide an indication of the many activities that children can pursue:

- *Special talks*
  - * Give opinions of stories.
  - * Give directions for a task described in a book (e.g. a magic trick).
  - * Talk on a particular topic.
  - * Interview a character from a story.
- *Monologues*   Assume the identity of a character in the story, and relate the story from a personal viewpoint (e.g. 'A day in the life of ...'), or relate another adventure involving the same chapter headings used in the book.
- *Discussions*
  - * Suggest alternative endings for a story.
  - * Consider the suitability of titles.
  - * Compare reactions of various children to a book or story.
  - * Compare and contrast similar stories.
  - * Compare events within a story with their own lives.
- *Oral reading, audience reading and drama*
  - * Prepare and read a favourite short story, to share an enjoyable experience with a classmate, group or younger class.
  - * Read a selected section of a story (an interesting, humorous or descriptive part).
  - * Read to provide information.
  - * Dramatise whole or part of a story.
  - * Dress up in costumes appropriate to a story.
- *Art and craft activities*
  - * Paint favourite characters from stories.
  - * Make wall murals and collages.

* Design and prepare illustrations for a story.

* Prepare maps, graphs and charts to illustrate talks on factual material read.

* Design and prepare a book jacket.

* Design and construct dioramas and other 3D forms, to illustrate sections of a story.

* Make character costumes and masks.

* Plan, design and prepare book displays on particular types of stories (e.g. science fiction, animal stories).

* Depict a story as a series of sequential pictures (cartoon).

* Compile a scrapbook on a subject (e.g. space travel, sport).

● *Experiences*

* Practise and sing a song related to a story (e.g. *Wizard of Oz*).

* Discuss moral dilemma situations related to a story.

● *Written activities*

* Prepare a summary.

* Prepare a story or book report.

* Make a filmstrip of a story. One group illustrates the development of the story, while another prepares captions and sentences. (Use old black and white filmstrips that have been wiped by dipping in bleach.)

* Write a story in his/her own words.

* Write original stories based on incidents or characters in a story.

* Write poetry, stimulated by stories or nonfictional material.

* Dramatise a story into a radio or stage play.

* Prepare an advertisement for a story, play, article or poem.

* Prepare a newspaper account of incidents in a story.

* Compile lists of questions on a piece of nonfiction material. Other class members answer the questions.

I have used all the above ideas and found them useful. However, remember that *the easiest way to stimulate interest in reading is to show that you value reading*:

● Read to children constantly.

● Read while they read.

● Gain a greater knowledge of childrens books by reading them regularly.

● Show a genuine interest in the books children have read.

CHAPTER SIX
Programming reading

While employed as a reading–language consultant, I worked with many class-room teachers. Their requests for help always took a variety of forms and covered an endless number of topics. However, a few questions seemed to crop up time and time again. One of the favourites was 'Please, can you help me with pro-gramming?'

This always seemed a reasonable request. After all, I remembered the count-less hours I had spent programming and the problems I had experienced with my first few programs. However, it always puzzled me that they had not managed to find a good reference book on programming to sort out their problems.

A quick review of the countless teachers reference books concerning the teaching of reading provided the answer. Very little *practical* advice has ever been outlined. Many books on reading totally ignore the question of programming, and those that do deal with the subject provide vague and sketchy suggestions that are of little use to any classroom teacher.

I suspect that the lack of good advice is in most cases due to the fact that the authors have rarely had to prepare a reading program. On the other hand, it may be that the subject is too difficult. After all, there are good reasons why it is difficult to outline a clear set of principles relevant for all teachers:

• The personal philosophy and methods used by different teachers have an obvious influence on the type of program designed.

• School policy on reading instruction often varies, leading to specific limitations that create further diversity (e.g. a schoolmistress may decree that reading shall not commence until term two in the first year of schooling).

• The expectations of parents vary from school to school, imposing restrictions.

• School organisational policy often imposes restrictions. The needs of teachers with graded, parallel, composite and ungraded classes vary, not to mention those of teachers in team-teaching situations.

• Children at different stages of development often require different approaches and therefore different programs.

• The type of reading materials available in the classroom often imposes limitations.

• Some classrooms and schools have different human resources. For example, some have greater access to resource teachers, peer tutors (e.g. in composite classes) and parent helpers.

• Finally, departmental curriculum statements may influence the program devised.

Nevertheless, there do seem to be a number of steps and guiding principles that have relevance for all teachers.

What are the steps to programming?

Step 1: Assess needs   This should involve both formal and informal assessment methods. Often it is useful to begin with one or more standardised tests, before more thoroughly applying less structured methods of assessment. Remember, this assessment should include consideration of interests, attitude towards reading, oral and written comprehension, word identification skills, oral reading (use miscue analysis), silent reading habits and study skills (for older children).

Step 2: Determine ability groups   While many different types of grouping will probably be used, ability groups are the starting point. A word of advice: the number of groups chosen should reflect your capacity adequately to teach them. *Remember, it is better to teach two groups well than four groups badly.* Try to handle the maximum number of groups you find 'comfortable'.

Step 3: Establish your priorities for each group   Carefully select a few goals based upon your initial evaluation. It is often better to restrict the number of goals, rather than attempt everything at once. These goals should be specific, achievable and, if possible, measurable (e.g. each child will read at least six books in recreational reading; each child will develop greater fluency and expression in audience-reading situations).

Step 4: Examine the materials available: 'Scratch' around every storeroom in the school; you may be surprised at what you find. Also, give some thought to the materials available outside the school (e.g. public libraries, books at home, newspapers, magazines).

Step 5: Determine the overall programming approach   Decide whether your approach will be fully integrated, partially integrated, basal, etc. Define the components of your program, and draw up a 'rough' weekly timetable.

The preceding chapters give ample indication of the content that should be in your program. Obviously, the timetable devised will vary, depending on the many influences discussed above. Nevertheless, three sample timetables are outlined on pages 84–88.

Step 6: Select appropriate learning activities   At this stage, the hard planning starts. This is obviously the core of your program. To make your job easier, use as many references as possible. It is at this stage that this book will probably be of greatest benefit. Perhaps also use other reference books, curriculum documents and basal-reading scheme manuals (if a basal scheme is being used).

Obviously, the activities selected will depend upon:
- the individual needs of your children;
- the overall approach(es) used; and
- the materials and resources available.

As a result, programs will vary greatly. Nevertheless, an attempt is made on pages 89–98 to outline three sample programs. While it is not possible (given space limitations) to outline each program fully, the core of each program is described.

Three sample timetables

Included on pages 85, 86 and 87 are sample timetables for Kindergarten, Year 2 and Year 5. (These are copyright free: the publisher grants permission for them to be photocopied.) Notes on the Kindergarten program appear below; those for the Year 2 and Year 5 programs appear after the timetables on page 88.

Notes on kindergarten program

The timetable opposite shows time slots with fairly general labels because of the nature of the program required in Kindergarten, where it is necessary to plan many varied activities each day. Hence, activities in the early-morning integrated-language sessions vary from day to day, although obviously there is some common pattern to the lesson sequence.

Integrated language activities   In this session, most activities are fully integrated language activities related to a central theme or experience. As such, children are talking, listening, reading and writing each day.

Literature   Two sessions per day are devoted to reading literature. Some of this is related to the central theme. However, other poetry, prose and drama also are selected, because of their special interest or style.

Reading activities   Children carry out a variety of reading activities, including the reading of simple books, sight word development, and prereading activities (for children needing them).

Daily writing   All children are encouraged to write. While some children will only draw (at first), this is still seen as a valuable activity. (See Chapter 2 for further details relating to this activity.)

Detailed programming for part of this timetable is given on pages 89–91.

Kindergarten (5–6 years): Integrated language

Time	Monday	Tuesday	Wednesday	Thursday	Friday
10.00 a.m. to 11.00 a.m.	.... Integrated language activities				
11.15 a.m. to 11.25 a.m.	.... Literature				
11.25 a.m. to 11.40 a.m.	.... Daily writing				
1.30 p.m. to 1.45 p.m.	.... Reading activities				
3.05 p.m. to 3.15 p.m.	.... Literature				

Year 2 (7–8 years): Integrated basal

Time	Monday	Tuesday	Wednesday	Thursday	Friday
9.45 a.m. to 10.00 a.m.	Language activities		............Language activities............		
10.00 a.m. to 10.30 a.m.		• Basal activities • Reading centres			• Basal activities • Reading centres
11.30 a.m. to 12.00 noon				Integrated activities	
1.30 p.m. to 1.45 p.m.	............................Recreational reading............................				
1.45 p.m. to 1.55 p.m.	............................Literature............................				

Year 5 (10–11 years): Individualised basal

Time	Monday	Tuesday	Wednesday	Thursday	Friday
10.30 a.m. to 11.00 a.m.	Basal activities ....(three groups).....................				
11.30 a.m. to 12.30 p.m.					Individual integrated-reading activities
1.30 p.m. to 1.40 p.m.	...................Literature....................			...................Literature....................	
1.40 p.m. to 2.00 p.m.	....Recreational reading...				
2.00 p.m. to 2.10 p.m.			Literature		
2.10 p.m. to 3.00 p.m.			Media studies		

Notes on year 2 program

The timetable is planned for three groups, using a total-language basal-reading scheme.

Language activities   These are related to one group's basal reader. The whole class shares in these activities. Each group has one lesson per week that is appropriate for its reader; other lessons are completed as part of the total group, because of their value for language.

Basal reading   The major reading session (10.00 a.m. – 10.30 a.m.) involves the use of three groups. One group does basal-related work, while others work at specific reading centres (e.g. taped readers, reading games, activity sheets). Each group receives four sessions per week.

Recreational reading   Everyone reads silently.

Literature   Teacher reads a variety of literature to the class.

Integrated activities   All children pursue activities from a variety of subject areas that relate to the theme of their basal readers. They have one session per week.

Detailed programming for part of this timetable is given on pages 91–95.

Notes on year 5 program

The timetable is planned for a combination of individual, whole class and group activities (using a basal scheme).

Basal activities sessions   Three groups pursue different activities (four lessons per week).

Recreational reading   All children read silently. Provision is made for individual conferences.

Individual integrated-reading activities   Individuals choose activities related to books read in recreational reading.

Literature   Teacher reads a variety of literature to class.

Detailed programming for part of this timetable is given on pages 95–98.

Kindergarten sample program (integrated language)

This program applies to term 2 of Kindergarten.

Timetable   As outlined on page 84.

Time period   At least three weeks. This may vary, depending on the extent to which specific activities are pursued.

Grouping

• Use the whole class for many of the integrated activities.

• Form special groups for some of the reading activities, according to need (e.g. prereading activities).

• Use ability groups for specific reading sessions (e.g. sight word development, reading of simple books).

• Individuals will pursue their own reading and writing in some sessions.

• Use social groups also for some integrated activities.

Reading activities   (15 minutes per day) Group activities for sight word development and reading readiness are outlined below, as well as suggestions for individual reading.

Integrated language activities   (1 hour per day) The activities outlined below are not allocated to specific lessons, because it is difficult to predict how long each activity will take. They are based on the central theme 'Toys are terrific' and the related experience of planning a toy show. (Further experiences are suggested in Chapter 2.)

Literature   (20 minutes per day) Suggestions for both theme-related and other literature are given below.

Daily writing   (15 minutes per day) Give each child a blank-paged book for writing, and each day encourage children to 'write' about something they are interested in. Some children will draw, while others will write words and sentences. Throughout this session, roam around the room, asking children about their writing and giving help and encouragement. Devote one period each week to sharing this writing.

LESSON	ACTIVITIES

Reading activities

• Sight word development (in three groups)

✪ Introduce words:
  * group 1: *see, play, can, jump, friend, book*;
  * group 2: *sister, brother, was, would, story, with, yes, no*;
  * group 3: *down, up, were, could, you, will, are, saw*.

✪ Use words in writing, making with plastic letters, sentence cloze and group games (see Chapter 3 for game suggestions).

• Reading readiness (three children only)

✪ Using a large print book, reinforce left-to-right sequence, as well as the concepts of word, letter and sentence.

✪ Children try to detect differences in sequences of words (e.g. *play, play, pley, play*).

✪ Ask children to complete sentence cloze using set sentence pattens (e.g. *I can . . .*).

• Daily reading (individuals)

✪ Encourage each child to read a book each day then take it home to read to parents. You might use some of the following series:
Methuen Instant Readers, Young Australia Caption Books, Reading Rigby (level 1), Methuen Caption Books, Methuen Jumpers, Breakthrough Readers.

Integrated language activities

• Preparation for toy show

✪ Outline to the class that a toy show is going to be held. Ask children to bring in their special or favourite toys.

✪ Categorise the toys (e.g. soft, mechanical, construction, dolls, electronic, funny, unusual). Discuss how the toys are alike and different.

✪ Design labels for the toys. Ask children to suggest labels that are funny, explanatory, imaginative, etc. (e.g. *Come and pat me. I won't bite*). Display the labels, and read them daily with children.

✪ Split the class into two groups to make posters advertising the toy show.

✪ Discuss the details required on an invitation to attend the toy show. Then:
  * prepare it on the board with the class giving suggestions;

• Follow-up to the toy show

* prepare a stencilled copy, which each child completes as a cloze exercise, filling in the names of the people to be invited and signing his/her names; and
* children each invite a child from another class and their parents.

⭐ Help the children design and make special award cards for the toy show winners. Make lots of them, so that all children will win a prize (e.g. smallest toy, most unusual toy, prettiest doll, noisiest toy).

⭐ Involve children in the preparation of the display (e.g. preparing signs to direct guests, ushering people around).

⭐ Children describe their favourite toys, giving reasons. Prepare a book titled 'My Favourite Toy'. Scribe each child's response, and let him/her illustrate it.

⭐ Ask children to design and draw a toy they would like to own. Place captions on the drawings, and display them around the room.

⭐ Discuss the sounds that some toys make, and produce a special book titled 'Bop, Whirr, Whizz, Bang'. Each child selects a toy, draws it and suggests a caption, which you then scribe.

⭐ Teach the following songs: 'The Marvellous Toy', 'The Teddy Bears' Picnic'. Use 'The Marvellous Toy' for reading, adopting a phrase-reading approach.

Further ideas of this type are outlined in Chapter 2.

Literature

• Theme-related literature

⭐ Examples are: *100 Chocolate Soldiers*, *Arthur's Honey Bear*, *The Teddy Bears' Picnic*, 'I Have a Lion' by Karla Kuskin (poem).

• Other literature

⭐ Examples are: *Terry's Brrrmmm GT*, *Fantastic Mr Fox*.

Year 2 sample program (integrated basal)

Timetable As outlined on page 88.
Time period Three weeks. (If programming is done over a longer period, add additional modules, like this one.)

Grouping   Divide the class into three groups:
- Use three groups for basal activities lessons like the ones outlined below.
- Use whole class grouping for basal language activities. Each group will join in the activities of all other groups.
- Use social groups also for integrated activities.
- Individuals will also pursue their own reading in recreational-reading sessions.

Programming using such an approach requires three separate outlines for the basal activities: one for each group. As an example, the activities for only *one* group (the middle group) are outlined below. The planning for other groups will be similar, but the reading material and specific activities will differ. An outline of the whole class activities is also given.

Recreational reading   (15 minutes each day, whole class) During this period, all children read silently. Allow them to find a comfortable position anywhere in the room. In this session, help children to select books, conduct individual conferences, and read with the children. (See Chapter 5 for further details on recreational reading.)

Literature   (10 minutes each day, whole class) During this period, read the class a variety of literature (e.g. *Amazing Mr Fox* (serialised), *The Lighthouse Keeper's Lunch*, *The Rainbow Serpent*, *The Paper Bag Princess*).

Basal program   (middle group) The program outlined below is based on the book *Pumpkin Paddy* (level 4 of the Reading Rigby program). Note that the integrated activities and language lessons are pursued by all class members (this can be varied by allowing other groups to do independent reading). This is done for organisational reasons. Where one of these sessions is timetabled, groups take turns having these activities based on their reader.

Reading centres   These are used by groups not engaged in basal-reading activities during the prime reading session. These centres are designed to allow children to work independently, so that you are free to work intensively with the group doing basal work. While they will vary throughout the programming period, they will include:
- taped readers;
- reading games (e.g. board games such as Snakes and Ladders, Motor Cross, Grand Prix);
- language puzzles (e.g. crosswords);
- oral audience reading;
- listening activities (e.g. oral comprehension using the listening post); Uand
- journal writing.

LESSON	ACTIVITIES

Basal program (middle group)
Week 1

1 Introduction to the reader (language activities)	✪ Read *Johnny Appleseed*. ✪ Discuss: 'What did Johnny Appleseed do as

wandered about the countryside?', 'Why did he plant apple seeds?', 'What sort of person must he have been?'

Further details relating to balanced questioning can be found in Chapter 4, pages 00–00.

2 Stimulus picture (basal activities)

✪ Show stimulus picture 25, 'Pumpkin Paddy'. This picture (and others) are provided with Reading Rigby. Examine picture with children. Discuss, using questions on reverse side (Observation and Comprehension sections). Select specific questions from those provided. Use Application section to draw a comparison between Pumpkin Paddy and Johnny Appleseed.

✪ Each child draws a picture of him/herself as a swagman.

✪ **Integration** Encourage children to bring some pumpkin or melon seeds to school (all groups may join in this activity). Prepare a class garden. Observe the germination of the seeds and the development of the vines. Children record their observations.

3 Word study (basal activities)

✪ Introduce difficult (or new) words: *about, flew, gone, night, people, talked, different, were, sow.*

✪ Introduce compound words: *billycart, bushfire, everybody, homestead.*

✪ Discuss words, use them in sentences, play a game (e.g. Buried Treasure, see page 30).

✪ Children complete a word study stencil.

4 Introduction of book (basal activities)

✪ Look at *Pumpkin Paddy* with children. Ask questions such as: 'What type of person do you think Pumpkin Paddy looks like?', 'Look at page 4. What is Pumpkin Paddy carrying?', 'Why would he need these things?', 'Is he coming, or going?', 'Would you like to be a swagman?', 'Why or why not?'.

✪ Children read the first story in the reader silently to find out what Pumpkin Paddy planted and why he grew his fruit and vegetables.

✪ Discuss story.

5 Thematic picture (integrated activities)

✪ 'Yesterday, some children read about a swagman and discussed whether they would like to be one.' Lead in this way to thematic picture 6, 'Me, Big and Strong' (provided with Reading Rigby). Discuss: 'What would you like to be when you grow up?'

✸ Children make a scrapbook of interesting jobs in the city and in the country.

✸ Read *The Barber* by C. J. Dennis. Look for other 'I'd like to be' poems.

✸ Revise sight words.

6 Oral reading (basal activities)

✸ Children read 'Pumpkin Paddy the Swagman' orally. Group members read in pairs, attempting to use expression.

Week 2

7 Related phonics (based upon needs identified in previous programming period — basal activities)

✸ Introduce *oo* in *boot, cockatoo, shoo.*

✸ Read *Snoop the Moose* (Rigby Leapfrog).

✸ Find other *oo* words. Write them down, and discuss.

See Chapter 3 for further phonic activities.

8 Directed reading (basal activities)

✸ Discuss: 'Pumpkin Paddy was liked by children. Why were children always glad to see him?'

✸ Children read 'Paddy and the Children' silently.

✸ Discuss story.

9 Thematic picture (integrated activities)

✸ Explain to the class that the middle group is reading *Pumpkin Paddy*: 'Some of us had not heard about the vegetable squash before. There are probably other vegetables some of us have not seen.' Introduce, in this way, thematic picture 8, 'Red for Stop, Green for Go' (provided as part of Reading Rigby). Examine the vegetables and other food in the picture.

✸ Examine a variety of unusual vegetables you have collected.

✸ Children make a list of five foods they like best, and a list of foods they hate, then make a wall chart for each.

✸ Children make a collection of food labels, then use them for a collage.

10 Cloze exercise (language activities)

✸ Children use the words introduced and discussed last week to complete oral and written cloze (write sentences on the board).

11 Directed reading (basal activities)

✸ Read 'Pumpkin Paddy Stories' to find out about some of Pumpkin Paddy's brave deeds.

✸ Discuss: 'Are they all true?'

✸ Make up one together. Each child writes it on a sheet of paper, then illustrates it.

12 Oral reading (basal activities)

✸ Children read selected sections of 'Pumpkin Paddy Stories' orally, and dramatise them.

Week 3

13 Related phonic work (basal activities)

✪ Introduce *oo* as in *good, kookaburra, wood*.
✪ Read *A Cook for Captain Cook* (Rigby Leapfrog).

14 Audience reading (basal activities)

✪ Children read the story 'Paddy Needs Help' orally.
✪ Children practise reading pages 19 and 20 out loud.
✪ Individual children (volunteers) read to group.
For ideas on audience reading, see Chapter 5.

15 Thematic picture (language activities)

✪ Explain that the middle group has been reading *Pumpkin Paddy*. Discuss: 'Poor Pumpkin Paddy had an accident and broke a leg. If you broke your leg, what would happen to you?', 'What would the doctors do?'
✪ Introduce thematic picture 6, 'Under Things' (provided by Reading Rigby).
✪ Children dramatise the story 'Paddy's Accident', and accidents other people have had.

16 Directed reading (basal activities)

✪ Children read 'Paddy's Accident' again, silently.
✪ Ask children to recall the major details of the story. Write them on the board in point form.

17 Song (integrated activities)

✪ Introduce the song 'Pumpkin Paddy' by Alex Hood.

18 Cloze exercise (basal activities)

✪ Children complete a cloze exercise based on the first two pages of 'Paddy's Accident' (eighth-word deletion). (See Chapter 4 for details on the preparation of cloze passages, pages 58–60.)

Year 5 sample program (individualised basal)

Timetable   As outlined on page 88.
Time period   Three weeks. (If programming is done over a longer period, add additional modules, like this one.)
Grouping   Divide children into three groups:
• Use three ability groups for basal activities.
• Individual reading will occur in the recreational-reading sessions and integrated activities session.
• Use social or skill grouping for media studies.
While separate programs are required for each group, only *one* group's program

(the middle group's) is outlined below. General outlines are given for whole class activities also.

Recreational reading   (20 minutes each day) Devote a daily session to silent reading. Each child is required to select a position anywhere in the classroom and read by him/herself. Conduct individual conferences, read with the class, and help children with book selection.

Integrated reading activities   (1 hour per week) This one-hour session provides an opportunity for children to create something related to a book they have been reading during recreational reading sessions. Encourage children to select a variety of activities. They may:
• prepare a monologue based on an adventure in a story;
• suggest (and write) an alternative ending for a story;
• prepare a favourite part of a story for presentation to the class (audience reading);
• paint a picture related to a book;
• create a model depicting a scene in a story; or
• prepare a dramatised version of part of a story.
(Additional integrated-reading activities are outlined in Chapter 5, pages 80–1.)

Media studies   (50 minutes per week) In this weekly session, children pursue a specific topic, as a class. Usually, they work in groups (social or skill). For the three-week period in the program outlined below, children look at newspaper and magazine advertising.

Basal activities   (middle group) The program outlined below is based on the book *Smithy* (level 8, Reading Rigby scheme). This book contains a number of short stories about Charles Kingsford-Smith. Note that the language activities are experienced by the whole class. Groups each have a turn (in the normal cycle of their basal programs) to have their story used for language work. This is seen as a valuable language lesson for all children and as an excellent way to unify the class.

LESSON	*ACTIVITIES*

Media studies (whole class)

1 Familiarisation activities (week 1)	✪ Children cut out advertisements (both feature and classified) from newspapers and magazines they have collected.
2 Advertising analysis (week 2)	✪ Children examine these advertisements and look for similarities. Ask them to categorise the advertisements. ✪ Discuss the categories formed. It is likely that they will be grouped only by product type. If so, attempt to lead the class to realise that different approaches are used in different advertisements. ✪ Point out some appeal factors, and discuss

how they work (e.g. 'Scientific tests have proven
. . .', 'You should use only the best for your
family . . .', 'Everyone uses . . .').

⊛ Ask children to think of television advertisements that use similar appeal factors.

⊛ Children categorise all the advertisements
cut out, according to the specific appeal factors.

3 Writing activities
(week 3)

⊛ Children each attempt to write an advertisement, using a specific appeal factor.

Basal activities (middle group)
Week 1

1 Introduction to the theme
of the reader (basal activities)

⊛ Introduce the concept of exploration.

⊛ Discuss relevant questions:
* What is an explorer?
* What qualities does an explorer have?
* Can you name some explorers?
* What did these explorers do?
* What problems did they face?
* Many other people (not explorers) have had
this same spirit of adventure. Who were/are
some of these people? What did they do?

⊛ Children perhaps read a biographical story
about a well-known explorer.

2 Introduction of book
(basal activities)

⊛ Show the book. Look at the cover together.
Ask questions like: 'This is the same spirit of
adventure we talked about yesterday. What do
you think they might have done?', 'What might
it have been like to take part in this adventure?',
'Can you think of some modern day people with
similar goals (e.g. scientists working on space
shuttle)?'

⊛ Read pages 7–9 to the class. Allow the middle
group to read on to page 14. Ask them to look for
interesting or difficult words.

3 Word study (basal activities)

⊛ Examine words children have indicated from
previous lesson. This may involve:
* derivation of words (e.g. *Southern Cross*, *navi-
gator*);
* meaning in context (e.g. *pressure* [on
throttle]);
* structural analysis (e.g. *uneventfully*); and
* unusual or invented words.

Additional ideas for vocabulary development
can be found in Chapter 3.

4 Reading for a purpose (basal activities)

✪ Ask children to read silently up to page 11 to find out who helped Smithy to launch his expedition: 'How did they help?'

✪ Alternatively, ask children to read up to page 19, thinking about Smithy as they read: 'What sort of person was he?' Ask children to be prepared to list some of his characteristics when they finish.

Week 2

5 and 6 Reading for a purpose: audience reading (basal activities)

7 Comprehension (basal activities)

✪ Children practise reading pages 8 and 9 (lesson 5) for presentation to the group or class (lesson 6).

✪ Provide some balanced oral questions: literal, interpretive, critical and creative.

✪ Children complete written activities in the Rigby comprehension book (level 8).

8 Cloze exercise (basal activities)

✪ Select a double page, and remove every eighth word, concentrating on content words. Children complete the cloze exercise.

See Chapter 4 for further ideas and details on cloze exercises.

Week 3

9, 10 and 11 Language projects (basal activities)

✪ Children plan and carry out language projects in these three lessons, such as:

   * think of the names of other famous aircraft (maybe just craft) and write why these are chosen;

   * write a congratulatory telegram;

   * draw up and fill in a log book to indicate events on the journey;

   * write a newspaper story concerning the arrival of the Southern Cross; and

   * prepare a schedule for interviewing Smithy when he arrives at his destination (and perhaps present the interview to the class, with a partner).

✪ If these topics do not prove suitable, allow children to plan their own language project.

12 Independent reading (basal activities)

✪ Introduce the class to other books with a similar theme. Read some extracts, then perhaps encourage children to finish the books (e.g. *Around the World in Eighty Days*, *Journey to the Centre of the Earth*).

✪ Discuss the similarities between these adventures and Smithy's.

Some final thoughts on programming

Clearly, programming is a fairly demanding part of your responsibilities. It requires a great deal of time and thought to arrive at a program that is of use to you. However, there is little doubt that, if you can plan and program effectively, you will teach more effectively.

A few final *do's* for programming:

- Provide clear achievable goals (not too many).
- Provide balanced content. (This book aims to help you to attain this balance.)
- Allow for flexibility. (Do not be frightened to vary the program, e.g. when an experience leads spontaneously to some stimulating language work.)
- Provide a clear structure to your program. (Avoid 'War and Peace' programs that consist of 10 centimetres of collected sheets and resources.)
- Provide sufficient activities (or ideas) for the time period specified.
- Include a variety of activities and approaches within your program.

The purpose of this book has been to help you to cater more effectively for the reading needs of all children in your care. The program is an essential tool to ensure that you do just this. A well-designed and well-prepared program is a real asset to teachers of reading. Always ensure that your program *is* an asset by applying this simple test. Ask yourself:

- Do I use my program?
- Does it help me to teach reading?

If the answer to both these questions is 'No', throw the program away, and start again.

REFERENCES

Adams, M. J. (1980), 'Failure to Comprehend and Levels of Processing in Reading', in R. J. Spiro, B. C. Bruce and W. F. Brewer (Eds), *Theoretical Issues in Reading Comprehension*, Lawrence Erlbaum Associates, Hillsdale (N.J.).

Anderson, R. C. and Freebody, P. (1979), *Vocabulary Knowledge* (Tech. Rep. No. 136), Urbana: University of Illinois, Center for the Study of Reading.

Bierwisch, M. (1970), 'Semantics', in J. Lyons (Ed.), *New Horizons in Linguistics*, Baltimore: Penguin Books.

Carroll, J. (1976), 'The Nature of the Reading Process', in H. Singer and R. B. Ruddell (Eds), *Theoretical Models and Processes of Reading*, 2nd Edition Newark (Del.): International Reading Association, pp. 8–19.

Clay, M. M. (1975), *What Did I Write? Beginning Writing Behaviour*, Heinemann, Auckland.

de Bono, E. (1973), *Cort Thinking*, Direct Education Services, London.

Durkin, D. (1972), *Phonics, Linguistics and Reading*, Teacher's College Press (Columbia University), New York.

Gates, A. I. (1937), 'The Necessary Mental Age for Beginning Reading', *Elementary School Journal*, 37, pp. 497–508.

Goodman, K. S. (1975), 'Do you have to be smart to read; Do you have to read to be smart?', *The Reading Teacher*, vol. 28, 7, pp. 625–32.

Goodman, K. S. (1976), 'Behind the Eye: What Happens in Reading', in H. Singer and R. B. Ruddell (Eds), *Theoretical Models and Processes of Reading*, 2nd Edition, Newark (Del.), International Reading Association, pp. 470–96.

Goodman, K. S. and Smith, F. (1973), 'On the Psycholinguistic Method of Teaching Reading', in F. Smith (Ed.), *Psycholinguistics and Reading*, Holt Rinehart and Winston, New York, pp. 177–182.

Goodman, K.S. (1973), 'Miscues: windows on the reading process', in K. S. Goodman (Ed.), *Miscue Analysis: application to reading instruction*, Champaigne, Urbana, Illinois, ERIC Clearinghouse on Reading and Communication, N.C.T.E.

Goodman, K. S. (1973), 'Psycholinguistic Universals in the Reading Process', in F. Smith (Ed.), *Psycholinguistics and Reading*, Holt, Rinehart and Winston, New York, pp. 21–27.

Gough, P. B. (1976), 'One Second of Reading', in H. Singer and R. B. Ruddell (Eds), *Theoretical Models and Processes of Reading*, 2nd Edition Newark (Del.), International Reading Association, pp. 509–35.

Graves, D. H. (1981), 'Patterns of Child Control of the Writing Process', in R. D. Walshe (Ed.), *Donald Graves in Australia*, P.E.T.A., Sydney.

Heckelman, R. G. (1969), 'The Neurological Impress Method', *Academic Therapy*, 4, pp. 277–82.

Iran-Nejad, A. (1980), *The Schema: A Structural or A Functional Pattern* (Tech. Rep. No. 159), Urbana: University of Illinois, Center for the Study of Reading, February.

Johnson, D. D. (1971), 'A Basic Vocabulary for Beginning Readers', *Elementary School Journal*, Oct., pp. 31–33.

Kolers, P. A. (1972), 'Experiments in Reading', *Scientific American*, 277, pp. 84–91.

La Berge, D. and Samuels, S. J. (1974), 'Toward a Theory of Automatic Information Processing In Reading', *Cognitive Psychology*, 6, pp. 293–323

Levin, H. and Kaplan, E. L. (1970), 'Grammatical Structures and Reading', in H. Levin and J. Williams (Eds), *Basic Studies in Reading*, New York, Basic Books.

Mandler, J. M. and Johnson, N. S. (1977), 'Remembrance of things parsed: Story structure and recall, *Cognitive Psychology*, 9, pp. 111–151.

Neville, M. H. and Pugh, A. K. (1976–1977), 'Context in Reading and Listening: Variations in approach to cloze tasks', *Reading Research Quarterly*, 12, pp. 13–31.

Robinson, F. P. (1961), 'Study Skills for Superior Students in Secondary School', *The Reading Teacher*, 37, pp. 29–33.

Rumelhart, D. E. (1980), 'Schemata: The Building Blocks of Cognition', in R. J. Spiro, B. C. Bruce and W. F. Brewer (Eds), *Theoretical Issues in Reading Comprehension*, Lawrence Erlbaum Associates: Hillsdale (N. J.).

Schank, R. C. (1975), 'The Structure of Episodes in Memory', in D. G. Bobrow and A. Collins (Eds), *Representation and Understanding*, New York, Academic Press.

Schank, R. and Abelson, R. (1977), *Scripts, Plans Goals and Understanding: An Enquiry into Human Knowledge Structures*, Hillsdale (N.J.), Lawrence Erlbaum.

Smith, F. (1973), *Psycholinguistics and Reading*, New York, Holt, Rinehart and Winston.

Smith, N. B. (1970), 'Many Faces of Reading Comprehension', *The Reading Teacher*, vol. 23, no. 3.

Spiro, R. J., Bruce, B. C. and Brewer, W. F. (1980), *Theoretical Issues in Reading Comprehension*, Hillsdale (N.J.), Lawrence Erlbaum.

Stein, N. and Glenn, C. (1977), 'An analysis of story comprehension in elementary school children', in R. O. Freedle (Ed.), *Discourse Processing: Multidisciplinary perspectives*, New Jersey, Ablex Inc.

Thorndyke, P. W. (1977), 'Cognitive structures in comprehension and memory of narrative discourse', *Cognitive Psychology*, 9, (1), pp. 77–109.

Venezky, R. L. and Calfee, R. L. (1970), 'The Reading Competency Models and Processes of Reading', in H. Singer and R. B. Ruddell (Eds), *Theoretical Models and Processes of Reading*, Newark (Del.), International Reading Association.

Webber, B. L. (1980), 'Syntax Beyond the Sentence: Anaphora', in R. J. Spiro, B. C. Bruce and W. F. Brewer (Eds), *Theoretical Issues in Reading Comprehension*, Lawrence Erlbaum Associates, Hillsdale (N.J.).

CHILDRENS LITERATURE

Are You My Mother?, Eastman, P. D., Collins, London, 1962.
Arthur's Honey Bear, Hoban, Lillian, Scholastic Inc., New York, 1974.
Bear Detectives, The, Berenstain, S. and J., Collins, New York, 1976.
Charlie and the Chocolate Factory, Dahl, Roald, Puffin, Harmondsworth, 1979.
Charlotte's Web, White, E. B., Puffin, Harmondsworth, 1976.
Dr Dolittle, Lofting, H., Collins and Harvill, New York, 1968.
Fantastic Mr Fox, Dahl, Roald, Puffin, Harmondsworth, 1981.
Folk of the Faraway Tree, The, Blyton, Enid, Dean and Sons Ltd, London, 1972.
Island of the Blue Dolphin, O'Dell, S., Constable and Company, London, 1960.
Jennifer, Hecate, Macbeth and Me, Konigsburg, E. L., Puffin, Ringwood (Vic.), 1974.
Lighthouse Keeper's Lunch, The, Armitage, R. and D., Andre Deutsch, London, 1978.
Lion, the Witch and the Wardrobe, The, Lewis, C. S., Puffin, Harmondsworth, 1976
No Kiss For Mother, Ungerer, T., Methuen, London, 1974.
100 Chocolate Soldiers, Longridge, Bill, Lansdowne Press, Sydney, 1980.
Paper Bag Princess, The, Munsch, R. N., Scholastic Inc., New York, 1980.
Professor Branestawm, Hunter, Norman (Endeavour Reading Scheme, level 15), Bodley
    Head, London, 1972.
Rainbow Serpent, The, Roughsey, D., Collins, Sydney, 1975.
Summer of my German Soldier, The, Greene, B., Puffin, Harmondsworth, 1982.
Super Roo of Mungalongaloo, The, White, O., Puffin, Melbourne, 1980.
Teddy Bears' Picnic, The, O'Harris, Pixie, Golden Press, Sydney, 1978.
Terry's Brrrmmm GT, Greenwood, Ted, Ashton Scholastic, Sydney, 1980.
What Made Tiddalik Laugh?, Troughton, J., Nelson, Melbourne, 1977.
Where the Wild Things Are, Sendak, M., Bodley Head, London, 1973.
Wizard of Oz, The, Baum, L. F., Scholastic Inc., New York, 1958.

INDEX